RACING RON

WINNING AT THE TRACK AND LIFE

RACING RON

WINNING AT THE TRACK AND LIFE

RON TAYLOR

Published by:
Wilkinson Publishing Pty Ltd
ACN 006 042 173
PO Box 24135 Melbourne Victoria, Australia 3001
Ph: +61 3 9654 5446
www.wilkinsonpublishing.com.au
enquiries@wilkinsonpublishing.com.au

A catalogue record for this book is available from the National Library of Australia

Planned date of publication: 08-2021
Title: Racing Ron — Winning at the Track and Life
ISBN(s): 9781925927689: Printed — Paperback

Front cover photograph of Ron supplied by Kate Tyzack.
Photographs from Ron Taylor's collection, Colin Bull and *Truth* photographers John Murie, Alan (Spider) Funnel, John Keasing and others unidentified.

Design: Michael Bannenberg
Printed in Australia by Ligare Pty Ltd.

Lola loved animals, particularly cats and dogs. Here she makes friends with a Labrador in the little European country of Liechtenstein.

This book is dedicated to Lola, my wife of 49 years, my best friend and my staunchest supporter. So much of what is written here reflects her compassionate approach to life and her impish sense of humour. As I wrote these words I often felt her at my side, prompting here and there, giving me a nudge, or remembering some funny incident. It's her book as much as mine.

CONTENTS

Foreword

I never thought I would write a book about myself, or about my life, simply because I thought I had done nothing that would be of interest to anyone other than my own family.

But as the years have rolled on I thought my family might like to know what life was like when I was a boy growing up in Canberra, and how different the world is today compared to back then.

Because I was a sports journalist, my main working days were the weekend, so I didn't get much opportunity to spend time with my kids on the days when they were free, Saturday and Sunday.

It wasn't like that when I was young. Sunday mornings were special. That's when I would jump into bed with my dad and listen to his stories as a boy growing up in Melbourne. He would tell me of his visits to the Brunswick Baths where he learned to swim and won a medal for passing all the tests. And he would talk about places I had never heard of, like the Merri Creek, the Fitzroy Football Oval and Pearson Street in Brunswick, where he did an apprenticeship as a fitter and turner.

My kids never got to hear what life was like in World War II when I was only 11 and had to help my dad dig an air raid shelter in the backyard. And how hard it was for my mum to look after us on an airman's pay when my dad went to fight the Japanese.

They never knew how I, and my younger brother Norman, built a billycart out of a fruit box and pram wheels and lugged it all the way to Red Hill, about three or four kilometres from where we lived in Lockyer Street.

We gathered up broken branches and cut roots from trees with a tommyhawk until we had a load, then headed home, downhill, thank goodness. Firewood was scarce and dear, so those trips to Red Hill were a big help to mum with her budget.

My brother Norman and I also did early morning paper deliveries to earn pocket money to ensure we got to the movies on a Saturday arvo. If you thought that was easy let me tell you that handling papers in temperatures two and three degrees below zero was anything but fun.

This was a part of my life my children got very little opportunity to hear about, so I began to put a few notes down on paper in case some day they might express interest in family history.

As story followed story I began to realise some of the things I had done, and some of the things I had seen, could be of interest to others, and might even be helpful.

So I just proceeded along quietly to see where these stories were taking me and whether, indeed, they might make a book.

Well, thanks to the Coronavirus, now that I had so much time on my hands, it's been a pleasure to complete this tale of events that have made my life such a fortunate one.

I hope you find something to make you smile.

Ron

1

A Square Peg

'Taylor, you are a square peg in a round hole.'

This perceptive assessment of my performance as a clerk in the Department of Treasury in Canberra came from the Assistant Secretary, my boss, and, I have to say, he summed me up accurately.

Yes, I was out of my depth in the Treasury, posting figures from one big ledger to another, but it was my first job and suited me while waiting for something better to turn up. That chance came, and, when it did, it led me to a life of adventure, excitement and mystery as a racing writer.

I have always found throughout life that the best opportunities come through *people* you know rather than through *what* you know. In this case the people, or, rather, the person, was a footballer… a rugged defender playing for Eastlake in the Canberra Aussie Rules competition.

My team was Manuka, and we hated Eastlake.

It was a bit like the Carlton-Collingwood rivalry. Everyone in Carlton hates Collingwood… I think just about everyone in Melbourne hates Collingwood. It was much the same in Canberra. Manuka and Eastlake were adjoining suburbs and the rivalry was general, not just football.

Eastlake's back pocket player was a stocky, dark-haired dynamo called Tom Wharton. He was a thorn in the side to all the teams so we Manuka supporters hated Tom in particular. I had never met him personally, but I had booed him plenty of times on the field. Then, lo and behold, I found he was dating my cousin, Lorna. The sky was falling in!

Then I discovered that Tom was a senior official in Treasury and, theoretically, one of my bosses. Through Lorna he got to hear of my desire to become a journalist so he approached me at work one day and said he might be able to help. He knew the top brass in the Department of Information and he would have a talk to them.

Sure enough an offer came for me to transfer to Information. But there was a catch. The only suitable vacancy was in Melbourne with Radio Australia (a division of Information). I was 20 years old and had lived all my life in Canberra. But I was thrilled at the chance to go to Melbourne.

My father was born in Fitzroy and had told me many stories about growing up in Melbourne. How he used to swim at the Brunswick Baths, and walk to the Victoria Market. So the city held a certain fascination for me.

But first I would need his, and my mother's approval. We were a very closely knit family and home life with my mum and dad and two brothers was happy and loving.

I hadn't long turned 20, and my parents were worried about how I would cope in a big city. The population of Canberra had grown to around 14,000 at this time but it was still just a big country town, whereas Melbourne's population was getting close to 1,500,000.

Kids like myself who had grown up in Canberra had no idea of city life so I could appreciate my parents' concern. The problem was solved however when my father suggested that if his brother George, who lived in Melbourne, would take me in I could go. So Uncle George and Aunt Anne were contacted and, good people that they were, agreed to let me live with them.

2

The Italian Connection

But before I end this period in Canberra I should tell you some more of my early life there because it was so different to what young kids and teenagers experience in the cities today.

My dad was a blacksmith—not a horse blacksmith—he worked in a quarry and made picks and shovels and tools for various outdoor occupations like roadmaking or construction. He was as strong as an ox and at 16 was playing senior football for the Federals, the first Aussie Rules team in Canberra. It was later renamed Manuka in 1926.

By this time he had turned 20 and married my mother, Mary, a daughter of Peter Varena, the first Italian migrant to settle in Canberra. Peter's actual name was Pietro Varenna, but when he later became a naturalised Australian citizen, he anglicised it to Peter Varena.

Peter had seven daughters and one son, Peter. Finding husbands for all those girls might have presented a problem for some, but not to Peter (snr.) He opened a boarding house.

Before the Depression hit in 1929 there was plenty of work available in building the new capital, which created a need for accommodation for young men. This required young women to wait on the tables and do the laundry. That's where my mum and her sisters came in. They did all the work and were popular with all the young bachelors in the district, not only with those who lived in the boarding house but those, like my father, who visited.

Alcohol was banned in Canberra at the time and my dad was lucky enough to have a car which he used as a taxi to ferry people to Queanbeyan in New South Wales, where liquor was freely available. At 10 shillings a trip ($1) he made enough to marry my mother whom he had met at The Mess, as the boarding house was called.

Subsequently I was born in Queanbeyan, 12km away from Canberra, on 29 May 1928, a year after the Duke of York (who later became King George V1) opened Parliament House, now known as Old Parliament House. There was no midwifery section in the small Canberra Hospital at that time but the town of Queanbeyan was well established and had a modern hospital of its own.

It was the time of the Great Depression (1929-32) and things were tough for most Australians, very tough—more than a third of the population was unemployed. In Canberra all work had virtually ceased on the construction of the new capital city.

But my dad was more fortunate than most, he was working on a one day on, one day off basis. It wasn't enough to pay the rent on our cottage in Westridge (now Yarralumla) so we moved in with my grandparents in the suburb of Barton. My grandfather was a supervisor with the Department of Works and he had steady employment, luckily for us.

Barton was one of the earliest suburbs of Canberra, and, to my mind, one of the nicest. It was close to everything that mattered in Canberra at that time… Parliament House and Hotel Kurrajong, where many of the politicians stayed when the House was sitting. The administrative offices of West Block and East Block, and the shopping centres at Manuka and Kingston were nearby.

Things were so tough in those days when I was three or four

years of age, that a birthday present would be a pencil case with two or three HB pencils and a lined exercise book, and maybe a bag of marbles. So I learned to write at an early age.

Grandfather's house, in Young Street, was close to the Telopea Park School and I couldn't get there quickly enough. Strange, because most kids hated school. But I loved it.

Every morning (well, some) I would pretend I was going to school. I was four and my mother would cut me a sandwich for play lunch. I would head off full of courage but generally get only as far as the corner, eat the sandwich and return home.

But one morning I kept going right up to the school and into the building. I walked along a corridor and into a classroom where children were sitting at their desks. My memory is still clear as a bell on this time and I recall the teacher saying: 'Hello, what are you doing here.'

'I've come to school,' I said.

'Well you can sit at that desk while I write a note for your mother,' the teacher replied. 'You take this to her and tell her to send you back when you are five.'

This incident, I think, showed I had an adventurous spirit from an early age, a trait that led me to my ultimate position as Racing Editor of *Truth*, a post I held for 34 years.

So where did my love for racing come from? There was no family connection with horses, but my father liked a punt and I would run his bets to the local SP. I was 12 or 13 at the time and I was fascinated by the names of the horses, Lucrative, Beau Vite, Ajax, High Caste, Yaralla, Flight, Tranquil Star and All Love, all of them outstanding horses in the 1940-43 era.

I stopped running the bets when my dad joined the RAAF and was posted overseas in 1943, but it didn't stop me listening to the races. I particularly enjoyed the dramatic descriptive nasal tones of Ken Howard who broadcast the Sydney races, and had visions of myself becoming a racecaller.

I would hold an empty glass up to my mouth and call an imaginary race, the glass helping me to achieve that nasal quality that made Howard's descriptions so appealing to me. Later on I did call professionally, but that's another story.

During those early years of World War II when my dad was serving on Morotai Island to the north of Australia, I kept him informed of the racing and sporting news at home by making a pretend newspaper out of a sheet of A4 writing paper.

I would fold it into four by cutting along the folds so that you had four pages. Then I would rule the pages into columns and a write a story in each one, the main news on the front with a headline just like you would see in a real newspaper. I think this was when I first started to think about becoming a reporter.

A reporter to me was someone who wore a trench coat and a snap-brimmed hat, smoked cigarettes and looked like Humphry Bogart or Spencer Tracey. This image appealed to me, and, as my education progressed, I made sure I did well in English, concentrating on compositions and spelling. So at 17 I got my Leaving Certificate from the Canberra High School and started looking for a job.

There was only one newspaper in Canberra, the *Canberra Times*, and it already had a cadet reporter, my cousin Neville Prendergast, who passed his Leaving Certificate the same year I did. I had no idea that Neville was interested in journalism and, I'm sure he didn't know that I was. So it was quite a coincidence that we both sought out the same profession, and even more remarkable that we both became Racing Editors of metropolitan newspapers, Neville at the *Daily Telegraph* in Sydney and me at *Truth* in Melbourne.

So I had to look outside the square… that is, outside Canberra if I still wanted to be a reporter. I did, so I began writing to newspapers all around the country. The response was very limited but I did get offers of jobs with newspapers at Horsham and Dimboola in Victoria. I would have liked to take up the Horsham offer but my parents considered I was too young to leave home and fend for myself in a strange country town.

That left me with few options. There was little employment in Canberra unless you joined the Public Service, or became a tradesman, or worked in retail or hospitality, or in some business institution like a bank or an insurance company. I decided on the Public Service and, thankfully, my application to join was accepted.

Ron's grandfather Pietro Varenna with Aunt Sarah.

3

Reg Ansett Liked A 'Craven A'

Whoever made the decision to choose the Department I should work in considered I was best suited to Treasury. Heaven knows why, as mathematics was my poorest subject at school. Nevertheless I was appointed to a division of Treasury called Capital Issues. A funny thing happened there.

Capital Issues controlled the issue of shares held by companies registered on the Stock Exchange. If a company wanted to raise money it needed the approval of the Federal Government.

I worked in a small office which I shared with my boss, a former Melbourne man who had worked for the Perpetual Trustee Company in Collins Street before taking on this more prestigious job in Canberra. He had the power to say 'yes' or 'no' to a company's application.

On one particular day around 1947, a tall distinguished looking man was ushered into the room and took up a chair opposite the boss. From my small desk on the other side of the room I observed the man take out a packet of cigarettes and offer one to the boss. My boss loved a cigarette, particularly Craven A's, and they were very hard to come by as tobacco was rationed at the time as a wartime measure.

They lit up and the boss called out to me: 'Taylor, bring me the Ansett file will you'. So I hurried out to the File Room which contained hundreds, maybe thousands of files, all in manila folders and stacked row after row in a series of shelves that reached from floor to ceiling. They were all in alphabetical order so it wasn't hard to find the one labelled 'Ansett'.

It was quite a bundle but I lugged it back to office and stood before the boss.

'Taylor, this Mr. Reginald Ansett of Ansett Airlines, would you put his file down… there,' indicating a particular place on his desk, right on top of Mr. Ansett's packet of cigarettes. I did as I was told and resumed my place across the room.

When the interview was over and Mr. Ansett had left my boss called me over. 'Taylor, you can take the file back now.'

When I lifted the file up the boss said: 'Well, look at that now. Ansett has left his cigarettes behind. Care for a Craven A Taylor?' No fool my boss, Mr. Hunter.

I was restless at Capital Issues. It wasn't the kind of job I had planned for. I tried to join the RAAF when I turned 18 but the war had ended the previous August and they weren't interested in new recruits. So I enrolled at the National University to do night classes and study for a degree in Commerce. That was the only way you were going to get on in the Public Service. You needed a University degree.

But I found the University hours interfered with my football training. You were left pretty much to yourself to do the necessary study, so different to school where everything was more regulated. So when the exams came at the end of the year, I hadn't done the work required and consequently failed my subjects.

Some of my early memories of Canberra are of events and situations that just don't happen today. For instance, there was Empire Day on 24 May when all the kids bought crackers and let them off at a bonfire that night. Gone now.

Empire Day has been replaced by Labour Day, in March,

no crackers, they're banned. You could buy a Nestles chocolate for a penny. It was a thin rectangular piece of milk chocolate wrapped in silver paper and contained in a pretty red and gold wrapper. We kids got great enjoyment taking a penny and covering it with the silver paper so that it looked like a two-shilling piece (20 cents). Everyone was a wake-up to it, but in those days there were no electronic games to amuse kids so we had to invent our own fun.

School days at Telopea Park were pretty uneventful but a highlight for me was Melbourne Cup day. The Cup was generally run at 3.30pm, the same time as we were let out of class, so I had to run like mad to the nearby Kingston shops to listen to Jim Carrol's description coming from the local radio store.

There was always a big crowd gathered there and I would have to push through among the adults to get a good position to hear. I was familiar with the names of some of the runners because my dad liked a bet, and, in the days leading up to the race, I would overhear conversations with his friends when names like Peter Pan, Hall Mark, Shadow King, Allunga and Young Crusader would all be thrown up as contenders.

The first Cup I remember was won by the 100/1 shot Wotan in 1936. He beat my dad's fancy Silver Standard by a neck in a thrilling finish which had the big crowd in front of the radio shop in a pitch of excitement. I didn't realise it at the time but I guess that's where my interest in racing began.

4

The Prime Minister's Lodge

By the time I was 16 I wanted to be a jockey. I was light enough but starting to 'shoot up' as they say. Nevertheless I mentioned my hopes to the local newsagent, Mr. Scougall, for whom I worked before school delivering papers. Mr. Scougall was a racing man and a friend of the Sydney trainer Peter Riddle. Mr. Scougall wrote to Mr. Riddle outlining my age, weight and height and telling him I would like to be apprenticed to him.

At the time Peter Riddle was training the brilliant two-year-old Shannon, who later became one of the champions of the turf. In my schoolboy dreams I imagined myself riding this beautiful horse, even if only in trackwork. Unfortunately for me Mr. Riddle replied that I would become too heavy in a short time and that taking me on as an apprentice would not be practicable. I wasn't too disappointed though because, in my heart, I knew it was only a dream, and had it came to pass my parents would never have agreed anyway.

I enjoyed my time working at the Manuka Newsagency even though the winter mornings in Canberra were freezing and your fingers would get so numb that you couldn't fold the newspapers into the boomerang shape needed to throw them onto the customers' lawn or driveway.

I fancied myself a bit as an accurate thrower and this led

me to an unexpected meeting with the Prime Minister, Mr. Ben Chifley. It happened like this. Mr. Chifley lived in the Prime Minister's Lodge, a relatively imposing building by Canberra's modest standards, with a wide and roomy front porch leading to a heavy green entrance door.

The bell to announce visitors was smack in the middle of the door, round with a button protruding from the centre of it, an ideal target for me. Mr. Chifley didn't get just one paper, he got a bundle of them, and when all bound together they made a decent weight.

Mr. Scougall's mode of delivery was to drive a cut-down Morris Minor with all the papers contained in a big tea chest in the rear compartment. I would stand next to the tea chest, select the requisite paper, or papers, and throw them onto the premises as Mr. Scougall drove past. The Prime Minister's front door offered a unique challenge.

I reckoned that if I could hit the button on the bell it would ring and announce to Mr. Chifley that his papers had arrived. I had several tries, morning after morning, but mostly the papers fell short and ended up on the porch.

But this particular morning I put a bit more 'oomph' into the throw and the bundle flew higher and smashed into the overhead light fixture. There was an almighty crash of falling glass and then the screech of brakes as Mr. Scougall brought the car to a shuddering halt. I was petrified—well, probably 'shocked' would be a better word, at what I had done, and wondered what would happen next.

I didn't have to wait long. The front door opened and out walked Ben Chifley, straight out to the waiting car. Mr. Scougall was onto him straight away, full of apologies and offering to pay for the damage. But I needn't have been concerned. Mr. Chifley came right up to me, put his hand on my shoulder and said: 'Don't worry son, the Government will pay for that'. What a good bloke.

5

Football Was My Life

So now it's 1945, I am 17 and repeating Fifth Year at Canberra High School. I should have matriculated the year before but I failed the final exams. I couldn't believe it. I always passed exams. But on reflection I hadn't put in the work. I was football mad, playing rugby union for the school during the week and Aussie rules on Saturday.

That's right, my dad was a champion Aussie rules footballer but here am I playing rugby. How come? Well, the newly appointed Headmaster, Mr Watson, was a New South Wales man where rugby ruled supreme, be it League or Union. So he decreed that the only football the school would play was rugby union. A lot of Canberra people were unhappy with this decision, particularly those who came from Melbourne, but Alec Watson must have had friends in high places because he got his way.

Although I had never played union I actually became quite good at it, not because of any particular skill, but because of my physique. I was a very skinny kid and when I was 15 or 16 weighed only 8 stone 9 or 10 lbs, around 55 kilos. The teams in the competition were divided into weight divisions… Under 9 stone (57kg); Under 10 stone, and Over 10 stone (63.5kg).

Because I was so light for my age, I was playing in the Under 9 Stone division against boys aged 12, 13, and 14 and I had so much more experience than them. So it was no surprise I was one of the team's better players. I also had the added advantage that being an Aussie rules player I was adept at the drop kick, which is very useful in rugby because if you can do a dropkick over the crossbar that separates the two uprights of the goal posts it's called a field goal and is worth three points.

I used to take every opportunity to do the dropkick and my team built up quite a score that way. It really wasn't in the spirit of the game because you were supposed to score a try and earn five points, plus another two if you converted it with a place kick over the crossbar. But my thoughts were, if it's in the rules, go for it.

While rugby might not have been my cup of tea it was very popular with a lot of the boys and they were encouraged by the Headmaster who wanted the First XV to showcase the school's sporting achievements. He succeeded too because many of the players later formed the basis of the Canberra Royals, a premiership winning club in Canberra which produced some world class footballers, including seven who made the Wallabies.

One of the First XV players when I was in first year was a champion fella, Alan 'Ginty' Stevens. He was three years older than me and an all-round sportsman. He would be playing rugby for the school on Wednesday and Aussie rules for the Ainslie Football Club on Saturday. He caught the eye of the St. Kilda Football Club scouts and ended up playing two seasons from 1948 to 1950.

Another member of the St. Kilda team at that time was Fred Green, whom I had met in Canberra when he was playing for the Navy, a team representing the naval base at HMAS *Harman*, where Fred was stationed during the Second World War. I was 16 and getting the odd game with a combined Canberra team called City and would have played against Navy a few times.

Because of the war most of the able-bodied men in Canberra had gone off to fight the enemy and there just were not enough players left to keep up the regular teams like Manuka, Eastlake and Acton. So Canberra City was formed so the competition could continue. Anyone could get a game with City. You just had to turn up.

I should tell you a little about HMAS *Harman* because I always thought it was such a strange place to have a naval base. It was situated about 11km from Canberra's CBD just before you came to Queanbeyan. I thought it strange because the nearest seaport was 150km away at Bateman's Bay. But it made sense later when I learned that Harman was a wireless and communications facility and played an important role in the war by providing radio coverage for shipping in the Pacific Ocean.

Just after I had turned 20 and was in Melbourne working for Radio Australia, Fred Green had moved on to become captain of St. Kilda. I went to see him play at the Junction Oval, we caught up, and Fred invited me to come and have a training run with his team. It was one of the highlights of my brief football career. Playing kick-to-kick with men like Harold Bray, Keith Drynan, Ginty Stevens, Des Nisbet and Tom Meehan was magic for me.

So you can see football was a very big part of my life. At every opportunity I would be out kicking the 'Sherrin' after school and weekends, whenever I could. Failing my Matric in 1944 was a big wake-up call and, as I said, I had to go back and repeat the year. Fortunately I got the message, put my head down and got the desired result the second time.

My marks entitled me to a place at Melbourne University doing Veterinary Science, or at Sydney University doing Commerce and Economics, but I had no desire to leave Canberra at that point. I preferred to take a position in the Public Service and study at night for a Commerce Degree at the newly opened National University at Civic Centre.

I lasted only a year at the University and opted to drop out after failing my subjects.

Again I hadn't put in the necessary work and it became apparent I wasn't cut out for an academic career. I was more interested in sports of all kinds, and I liked reading about them. Journalism appealed to me.

It was lucky for me that Tom Wharton fancied my cousin Lorna and, through him, I was able to transfer from Treasury to the Department of Information which controlled Radio Australia.

6

Graham Kennedy Brought My Lunch

I'll never forget my last day in Canberra. My dad took me aside and handed me a 10 pound note ($20). 'This will help get you started,' he said. Ten pounds! A fortune for me at the time, and it must have been hard for my dad to part with because he wasn't earning very much himself.

To put this gift into perspective we had a crackerjack footballer in Canberra at the time, Johnny Hawke, who was three years older than me and playing senior football for Eastlake Aussie rules club on Saturday and for Canberra in the rugby league competition on Sunday. I don't know what Eastlake was paying him, but he was getting six pounds a game from Canberra for playing rugby.

When Johnny was selected to join the Australian Rugby League team to tour England in 1948 the Canberra Rugby League presented him with a gift of *ten pounds* to help him with his expenses. So how good was my dad!

Now I was ready to go. So down I went to the Canberra railway station to catch the train to Melbourne. There was no direct service from Canberra to Melbourne (still isn't) so I had to take the Sydney-bound train and get off at Goulburn and wait for the Melbourne Express to come through from Sydney.

What a send-off I had. My family, my mates from work,

some from the football team and other friends were all there. Some of the girls had made banners wishing me good luck and waved me good-bye until the train was out of sight. Next stop Melbourne.

I was greeted at Spencer Street Station by my Aunt Anne whom I had never met, but she soon found me and hired a taxi to take me to her home at No. 4 Glyndon Avenue in Brighton. I spent just over a year there with her family and they were among the happiest days of my life.

My duties at Radio Australia, which was situated at 475 Collins Street, were to listen to the overseas news broadcasts and record them onto a hollow wax cylinder, which was the way it was done back in those days. Then I would type up the material and it would go to the Editor who would decide if anything was newsworthy enough to be included in our own news bulletins.

After I had typed up my broadcast the cylinder had to be taken to another machine where it was 'shaved', that is, the recorded item was removed and the cylinder was ready to be used again. It seems an antiquated way of doing things by today's standards but it worked very well back in the 1940s.

The 'shaving' was usually done by the copyboy when he was wasn't running messages or out fulfilling the lunch orders. The copyboy I would hand the used cylinders to was a young fellow called Graham Kennedy, yes, the same one who became one of Australia's greatest television entertainers. It was Graham's first job and I just remember him as a shy little 15-year-old, a polite kid who did what he was told and who was popular with everyone in the office.

Graham didn't last long with us however and moved on to radio station 3UZ where he joined the record library. He got his first big break when the station's top personality Cliff Nicholls ('Nicky') needed a foil for his repartee and he thought Graham would be ideal as his straight man. They clicked and Graham went on to be a star on radio and later television. I must say I didn't see it in him when we worked together but it just highlights the old saying that you can't judge a book by its cover.

Another famous journalist who worked for Radio Australia—well, I thought he was famous anyway—was Frank Dexter, who was in the latter stages of his career after a distinguished innings as a racing writer for *The Argus*, a very popular Melbourne newspaper. Frank was the sportswriter for Radio Australia and would prepare the bulletins that would be broadcast overseas.

During the football season Frank would attend the main game, usually at the MCG. One afternoon he came back a little over refreshed and wasn't handling the typewriter too dexterously. So he called me over and said: 'I'll dictate and you'll type.' That was OK but there was still more to it than that. After the bulletin was prepared Frank had to take it to the ABC radio station a couple of blocks away in Lonsdale Street where he would get behind the microphone and read it out.

Because Frank wasn't travelling all that well I knew that wasn't going to happen. Frank knew it too so he says to me, 'You'll read the news.' I'd never been behind a microphone before, but always thought it was something I could do well. So here was my big opportunity. I must have handled it OK because Frank said to me later, 'That's what we'll do it in future, I'll give you the details, you'll type it up and do the broadcast.'

And that's the way it went. Frank was able to enjoy his Saturday afternoon at the football or the cricket and I was only too happy to add another talent to my meagre CV. I don't know what the Director of Radio Australia thought about our arrangement but as he never came into the office on a Saturday I doubt if he ever knew about it.

It's a funny thing in life the way opportunities come knocking. The incident with Frank Dexter gave me the confidence to treat the microphone as a tool that would help my career. A couple of years later I was calling football matches at Manuka Oval in Canberra.

Broadcasting of football was in its infancy in Canberra at that time and the broadcast 'box' was a kitchen table set up on the boundary line with two wooden chairs, one for me and one for my co-caller Tom McKernan who was brilliant with his descriptions of the play.

After the game I would be picked up by Len Mauger, one of Radio 2CA's announcers and driven to the station at Civic Centre where I would help him read the Sporting News. Len later became one of Australia's leading TV executives with posts including Managing Director and President of the Nine Network.

I enjoyed working in radio and later in life I did part-time stints on Radio 3KZ, 3UZ, and 3AW and was part of Channel 10's Melbourne Cup television coverage. Maybe there's a message there for all of us—never pass up an opportunity.

But before I move on to the next stage of my career, I'll tell you a little more of my life and times living in Glyndon Avenue and working at Radio Australia. I didn't realise it at the time but Glyndon Avenue, Brighton is one of the most fashionable streets in Melbourne in an area known as the Golden Mile. It wasn't recognised as such back in 1949 but from what I read in the real estate columns of the daily newspapers it certainly is now.

Glyndon Avenue runs off St. Kilda Street just after you pass North Road on the way to the Royal Brighton Yacht Club. It's quite a short street culminating at Port Phillip Bay and just a short walk from the iconic bathing boxes along the Dendy Street Beach.

A tram used to run along St. Kilda Street and that would

take me to the Olderfleet Building in Collins Street where Radio Australia had its offices. It was here that I wrote my first racing story. It was about the stallion Helios and broadcast all around the world, to wherever Radio Australia was being received—Britain, Europe, North America, Asia, and South Africa.

As they say in life, 'luck's a fortune' and I was lucky enough that my Uncle George, whom I lived with, was a good friend of Mr. E.A. Underwood, vice-Chairman of the Victoria Racing Club. Mr. Underwood was also the proprietor of Warlaby Stud, one of the showplaces of the Victorian breeding industry at Oaklands Junction, about 30km from Melbourne.

To get the story it was necessary for me to go Warlaby to see the stallion, who was quite unusual in that he had, in human terms, a clubfoot. This is a condition described by medicos as one that is normally applied to humans and is defined as a common malformation of the foot. The foot is bent in sharply so that the person (or animal), seems to walk on his or her ankle.

As I didn't own a car at that stage of my life Mr. Underwood drove me there himself and showed me over the property of which he was justifiably proud. He told me he had bought Helios from King George VI through the British Bloodstock Agency, expecting the horse to win some races before retiring him to Warlaby. Helios was beautifully bred by Lord Derby's champion Hyperion out of Foxy Gal by the four-time leading American stallion Sir Galahad III, and he became one of Victoria's leading sires.

Now, let me take up the story just as it was read out (in part) in Radio Australia's Sporting Diary program:

'But Helios was never destined to start in Australia. Taken to Flemington for exercise one morning he struck his near foreleg and suffered a compound fracture of the pastern. It was a nasty break

with pieces of the bone sticking through the skin. For six weeks it was touch and go with Helios. The injured leg was freely treated with sulphanilamide and eventually the colt pulled through.

'While the break was knitting—it was not placed in a plaster cast—the ligaments and the tendons of the foreleg drew up, causing the fetlock to knuckle over and giving the hoof a club-like appearance. To guard the leg Helios wears a special shoe with a steel bar attached to the front of the hoof so that when he walks the bar is in contact with the ground.'

Despite his disability I recall how surprised I was that Helios was still able to trot and canter, even if he did move with a queer bobbing action, his head nodding up and down. Although he was never destined to race Helios still proved a good investment for Mr. Underwood. He was Victoria's leading sire in 1949, the year his most famous son, Carbon Copy, won the Sydney Cup. It was a stellar season for Carbon Copy, his other wins including the AJC Derby, the W.S. Cox Plate, the St. George Stakes at Caulfield, the King's Plate at Flemington, the AJC St. Leger and the AJC Plate, which was run over 2 1/4 miles.

7

Off To The Country

They say lightning never strikes in the same place twice. But it did for me. It came about like this: After little more than a year at Radio Australia I felt I needed to broaden my experience as a journalist and began to look around for a job on a newspaper.

I tried the *Melbourne Herald* first because I thought I had a 'leg-in' there. One of the *Herald*'s chief executives was a man called Reg Leonard, I forget his actual title—probably it was Chief Of Staff. Reg had done a stint in the Parliamentary Press Gallery in Canberra and, while he was seconded there. he played football with the Manuka Football Club, which my father, Norman, captained and coached.

I knew Reg would remember my dad and I thought this would play in my favour when I applied for a job on his paper. Of course he remembered my dad—everyone in Canberra knew Norm, interstate representative, champion ruckman and champion bloke. But this didn't cut any ice with Reg. If I remember our conversation correctly, he told me every time he advertised for a cadet journalist he would receive 500 applications.

He told me he never considered anyone who wasn't a University graduate. So his advice was to get some experience on a country newspaper and build up a CV before trying the city again. I could tell he was sincere and trying to help so I thanked him for his advice and took my leave.

I applied to several country papers but had no luck until I came across an advertisement for a D-Grade journalist to join the *Cooma Monaro Express*, a bi-weekly publication based in Cooma, a small town about 100km from Canberra. Cooma appealed because of its proximity to Canberra, where my parents were still living.

Another advantage was that the Snowy Mountains Hydro Electric Scheme had just started up with its headquarters there, so it promised to be an exciting time for the town. Luckily for me my application was accepted and I signed on in January 1950.

The *Express* came out twice a week and was just a two-man band, the Editor, Mr. Walter Craigie, who was also the proprietor, along with Bill McGar, the linotype operator who doubled as a reporter and anything else required to get the paper onto the street. So when I joined we became a staff of three.

My main duties were attending Council meetings, the Pastures Protection Board meetings and some smaller local activities. Mr. Craigie looked after the Court and the more newsworthy stories. I also got to report on the local races, and that was the highlight of the job.

I would fill the whole back page of the paper, a broadsheet, so it was big—really big. I filled it by giving a ball-by-ball description of every race, detailed results, and stories about the horses and the personalities, the owners, trainers and jockeys.

Now all this is leading up to the reason lightning struck again and how I got another lucky break.

My arrival in Cooma on a Saturday afternoon was a lonely affair. The town was deathly quiet. The shops had closed except for a café or two and few people walked the streets. The population would have been less than 5,000 so I should not have been surprised.

I knew no one and had nowhere to stay. But being 21 and eager to start my new job on the Monday I booked into a hotel as a temporary measure before seeking more permanent accommodation. It didn't take long. My new boss, Mr. Craigie, was friendly with the proprietor of the local furniture shop who was prepared to take me in as a boarder. Stan Dykes was his name and he and his wife treated me like a son for the short period I was there.

As well as being a furniture salesman and a good bloke, Stan doubled as the racecaller for the Cooma Monaro race club. The races were held at the Ti-Tree Racecourse, about 6km out of town on the Numeralla Road. It was a typical country racecourse set in the middle of open paddocks, dry and dusty, but quite serviceable for the fields it catered for.

One race morning Stan came into the kitchen while I was having breakfast and croaked out that he had the flu and wouldn't be able to call the races that day. He said: 'Do you think you could do it?' Did I what! This was an opportunity I had dreamed about. So I replied I was pretty sure I could. I would be at the races anyway reporting for the paper and calling them wouldn't interfere. The fields were generally small, from say, five to ten runners depending on the class of race, so I was pretty confident I could handle it.

The first thing to do was to learn the colours of the silks the jockeys were wearing. Stan had given me his racebook and loaned me his binoculars. So I began to flick through the pages, studying the colours and repeating them over and over until I was fairly confident I knew them. But to make sure, before each race I would visit the jockeys' room and sit with the riders, who were all dressed up in their silks, and commit them to memory.

I got through the day without a hitch and when it was time

to pack up the chap in charge of the broadcasting system said he had been impressed with my performance.

'How would you like to come with me to other meetings where I set up the equipment?'

'Where would that be?' I asked.

'Well, Adaminaby, Bombala, Pambula, just around south-western New South Wales,' he replied.

I said I would be happy to as long as it was OK with Stan. He said Stan would be happy to give it up as it was only a hobby with him. So I started calling around the southern districts and I must have handled it OK because some of the locals began calling me 'the Ken Howard of the bush'. (Sorry for skiting.)

Eventually though I left Cooma. I really wasn't cut out for reporting court cases and council meetings, my interest was focused on sport. Mr Craigie gave me a nice reference to his friend John Shakespeare, the Editor of the *Canberra Times*, but even though my cousin Neville Prendergast had moved on to the *Daily Telegraph* in Sydney his place had been taken and there was no room for me.

So I was out of a job, but I had I still had one ace up my sleeve.

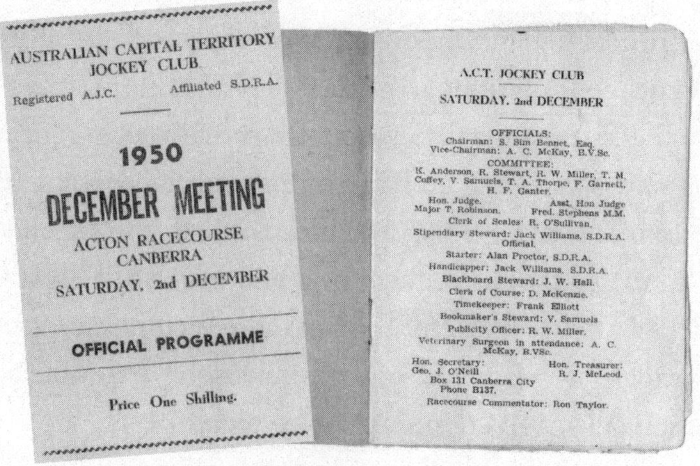

AUSTRALIAN CAPITAL TERRITORY
JOCKEY CLUB

Registered A.J.C. Affiliated S.D.R.A.

1950

DECEMBER MEETING

ACTON RACECOURSE
CANBERRA

SATURDAY, 2nd DECEMBER

OFFICIAL PROGRAMME

Price One Shilling.

A.C.T. JOCKEY CLUB

SATURDAY, 2nd DECEMBER

OFFICIALS:
Chairman: S. Sim Bennet, Esq.
Vice-Chairman: A. C. McKay, B.V.Sc.

COMMITTEE:
K. Anderson, R. Stewart, R. W. Miller, T. M. Coffey, V. Samuels, T. A. Thorpe, F. Garnett, H. F. Ganter.

Hon. Judge. Major T. Robinson. Asst. Hon Judge Fred. Stephens M.M.
Clerk of Scales: R. O'Sullivan.
Stipendiary Steward: Jack Williams, S.D.R.A. Official.
Starter: Alan Proctor, S.D.R.A.
Handicapper: Jack Williams, S.D.R.A.
Blackboard Steward: J. W. Hall.
Clerk of Course: D. McKenzie.
Timekeeper: Frank Elliott
Bookmaker's Steward: V. Samuels
Publicity Officer: R. W. Miller.
Veterinary Surgeon in attendance: A. C. McKay, B.VSc.
Hon. Secretary: Geo. J. O'Neill Box 131 Canberra City Phone B137.
Hon. Treasurer: R. J. McLeod.
Racecourse Commentator: Ron Taylor.

Racebook for the Canberra racemeeting in 1950 showing Ron as the Course Commentator.

8

The Southern Racing Guide

Before leaving Radio Australia, I was able to take 12 months leave of absence and this still applied when I left Cooma. As a temporary move (I hoped) I re-joined the Department of Treasury in Canberra. It was the same old grind and I was still restless. But now there was a glimmer of opportunity.

I found a way to use my time there usefully and it led to me getting my big break in journalism, a position on the influential Melbourne newspaper *The Argus*. How come? Well, I had built up some journalistic experience at Radio Australia and Cooma, and I was determined to continue in that profession if I possibly could.

So I made time between balancing Reconciliation Statements to start my own newspaper, *The Southern Racing Guide*.

Canberra had a handful of race meetings each year, held on the old Acton racecourse, now flooded to make way for Lake Burley Griffin. These meetings were well attended, up to almost 1000 people out of a population of just under 20,000.

Canberra people loved their sport and as well as being big followers of Aussie rules in Melbourne they were also big fans of racing in Sydney and Melbourne.

So when the races were on at Acton there was always a good turn up. But there was no form guide for the local races. There was plenty of information on Sydney and Melbourne from the interstate papers but nothing on the locals. I could see an opening for a form guide to cover the meetings at Canberra and Queanbeyan, the two meetings in the district that attracted the biggest crowds.

So I set about collecting the results of the all the races run under the banner of the South Western District Racing Association, which controlled the racing in southern New South Wales.

I bought a stack of lined index cards about 15cm x 10cm and wrote down the performance of each horse, the meeting where it ran, where it finished, it's price, where the others ran—all the details you would see in a metropolitan form guide like Sportsman or *Truth*. There was a card for each horse, listed in alphabetical order, and after a few meetings I had worked up a sizeable database.

It was laborious work and time consuming so I looked for a shortcut. I didn't have to search far. The answer was right under my nose.

I was friendly with the girls in the typing pool at Treasury, one in particular who was a neighbour. I explained my situation to her and she said there were occasions when things were slack at Treasury and she had time on her hands. She offered to help type up my cards when she got an opportunity.

It wasn't hard to explain the routine to her, all she needed was the cut out results of the race meeting from the newspaper and follow the style I had set out. Our arrangement didn't last long but while it did I was grateful for the assistance.

Once I had the form data base set up the next thing was to create a newspaper to contain it all—and to finance it. I had no savings, just my weekly wage from the Treasury. In those days the minimum wage was 8 pounds 2 shilling a week for an adult, and, at 22-years of age I wasn't even getting that much.

So I had to secure sufficient advertising to cover the cost

of printing. After work, and on weekends, I called on every shop in Canberra—at Kingston, Manuka and Civic Centre—no-one escaped me, the butcher, the baker, the barber, the jeweller, the chemist, the fishmonger, the newsagent, the grocer and all the rest. I explained what I was doing and said I wanted two pounds ($4) for a two inches by two inches (10cm x10cm) advertisement, more if the advertisement was larger.

Not everyone was interested, but I did get nine takers from among the business houses. Some were more generous than others. J.B. Youngs, the biggest store in Canberra selling everything from furniture to groceries, chipped in with a (25cm x20cm) ad and E.R. Snow Ltd., the big menswear shop, and the Hotel Kingston did the same. I was getting there but needed a little more.

The bookmakers were my next target. There were only eight on-course bookmakers operating in Canberra and Queanbeyan (but plenty of SP's), but to their credit everyone supported me. So I was right to go.

The first edition was set for the meeting at Acton on 1 January 1951. I designed a masthead calling the paper *The Southern Racing Guide*, I did the layout, wrote the copy and presented the lot to Mr. Shakespeare, the proprietor of *The Canberra Times*, to put it all together. He and his compositor Tommy Lowe, a former schoolmate of mine, did a magnificent job presenting me with a four-page tabloid that looked like a real dinkie-di newspaper—and that's what it was, a newspaper.

The next thing was to sell it. I distributed it among the newsagents and the hotels in Canberra and Queanbeyan and co-opted my young brother Don and two of his mates to stand outside the entrance to the racecourse and coerce everyone coming in to buy a copy. At sixpence (5 cents) a pop I wasn't asking much. The regular newspapers like the Sydney *Daily Telegraph* were charging 10 cents.

I think we sold nearly 200 papers that day. That brought in around 10 pounds, so after paying the boys their commission there wasn't much left. No that that worried me. The advertising had paid for the printing costs, and so long as the paper paid its way I was happy. My real object was to show what I could do as a journalist. And it worked.

After two more issues, one for Canberra and one for the races in Queanbeyan, I was ready to launch my attack on the Melbourne newspaper market. I had been a regular reader of *The Argus* when I worked for Radio Australia and admired the writings of Percy Taylor who covered the cricket, Hugh Buggy the football and Ken Moses, a hard-hitting columnist who could write on everything.

So *The Argus* was where I wanted to be. I gathered together all my material, copies of the *Southern Racing Guide*, the cuttings from the *Cooma Express* and the sporting commentaries I had compiled at Radio Australia and sent them all to the Sporting Editor with a letter expressing my desire to join the sporting staff.

I certainly felt I had the right credentials, it just needed for a vacancy at the paper to be available. Luckily for me there was. A couple of weeks later I received a letter from Mr. Nigel Balfe, the Sporting Editor, telling me that if I would come to Melbourne there was a job as a D Grade reporter on the general sporting staff.

GET THE BEST— IT COSTS NO MORE

Our Plant is operated by a Skilful and Well-trained Staff, so FOR THE BEST IN DRY-CLEANING GO TO— CANBERRA DRY CLEANERS

The Southern RACING GUIDE

EDITED BY: RON TAYLOR

CANBERRA

CANBERRA EDITION

FOUR PAGES. PRICE 6d.

MONDAY, JANUARY 1, 1951.

FIRE PATCH IN LINE FOR HAT TRICK

WINNER WAS REALLY "FLYING"

Success Will Earn Kembla Start

Should the locally owned and trained mare, Fire Patch, win the New Year's Day Handicap, one mile, principal event at Acton today, she will be taken to Kembla Grange on Wednesday to contest the Novice Handicap.

Trainer E. J. Gardiner mapped out this programme for the mare after she had convincingly won the C.R. & T.C. December Handicap, one mile, on this track two weeks ago.

The New Year's Day Handicap, worth £55, has attracted a better field than is usually seen at Acton and justifies the A.C.T. Jockey Club's policy, "better prize money, better horses."

Seven runners have been nominated, but scratchings are likely to reduce the field to five.

"The Guide" selections are: FIRE PATCH, 1; GREY SKY, 2; LEYTE, 3.

Fire Patch won four races in [illegible]

The mile will be new to him but trainer C. McDonald believes the gelding has the necessary stamina to be with the leaders all the way and expects him to go well.

Sir Donald is by Durham Ali (imp.) from Vampire, so is bred to run a middle distance.

LONG GALLOPS

An improving galloper with a place chance is Permanent, who will be ridden by A. Dudley. Permanent has shown plenty of [illegible]

With all four feet off the ground, Fire Patch (K. Browne) wins the C.R. & T.C. December Handicap, one mile, at Acton, 16th December, 1950. Prince Terry (N. Shard) is being eased down in second place, followed by Permanent (A. Dudley), and Sea Lord (K. Hemming). —J. Gillan Photo.

INTERMEDIATE HCP. ATTRACTS GOOD FIELD

The foresight of A.C.T. Jockey Club officials in substituting an Intermediate Handicap for a Flying Handicap [illegible]

FLOWERET COULD MAKE AMENDS

Mrs. J. B. Cooper's chestnut filly, Floweret, who failed to run a place when backed to favouritism at Acton on 2nd December, 1950, could make amends by winning the [illegible]

Standard. Another locally trained horse, Coronation Flag, was 9th in the same race.

Silver Remove will again be ridden by F. McNamara.

Little Chief, although he won a Maiden Handicap at the last meeting on this track, appears to be covered by Floweret, who beat him so easily at Goulburn.

In two starts this season Lee March has given no indication of producing the form which [illegible]

9

Hairy, Scary Times At *The Argus*

Journalists were graded according to their ability. You started off as a cadet, and after four years of training were promoted to D Grade. I was earning around ten pounds ($20) a week, which doesn't sound much these days but back then it was sufficient to pay for a room at the Post Office Hotel in Elizabeth Street where I stayed when I first arrived.

I didn't stay there very long, not because it wasn't a good hotel but, as its name implied, it was right next door to the GPO which had an enormous clock tower like Big Ben that rang out the hours in such a booming tone it was impossible to get a good night's sleep. After a couple of weeks I answered an advertisement for a 'Room To Let'.

I was successful in my application but it didn't turn out to be the right option. The house was owned by a married couple who differed significantly in age. The wife was about 30 and the husband at least 20 years her senior. The husband would leave for work early and I was left alone in the house with the wife until I had to start work at 2pm.

I soon got the impression that the husband didn't think that was a good idea, even though I was only 23 and not much more than a raw young kid.

So I decided discretion was the better part of valour and

quit before I got the heave-ho. The next venture into a Room to Let was much more successful. This time the landlady was an elderly widow who lived in Waverly Street, Essendon, not far from where *The Argus* Racing Editor Jack Elliott lived in Flower Street. This was most convenient for me as Jack would often pick me up and drive me to work and drop me home.

Jack wasn't much older than me, he was 30 and the youngest Racing Editor Melbourne had known. Jack was a good journalist, hard-hitting and fearless. He wasn't popular with racing officials because he wasn't afraid to criticise them, but he did have their respect.

One of Jack's regular targets was the VATC, the Victorian Amateur Turf Club (now the Melbourne Racing Club), which controlled Caulfield Racecourse. Whenever writing about the club Jack would put the stress on the word *Amateur* which used to rile the Chairman Sir Norman Robinson no end. But he was a good sport and often recognised that Jack had made a good point.

I didn't really get to know Jack until I had been at *The Argus* a few months because my first job there was as a general sports writer. I covered a little of everything, mainly cycling, board track racing as well as road racing. I had never seen board track racing and soon became a great fan. The events were staged at night at North Essendon (the track is long gone).

The stars were Billy Guyatt and Sid Patterson who had some stirring duels that made for exciting copy. Bike racing would attract crowds of up to 7,000 which made it a major sporting attraction. I enjoyed writing about the wide variety of sports but after about six months that all changed.

Our trotting writer, Bill Healy, received a better offer from *The Age* and defected. Before he left the Sporting Editor called me in and told me I would be the new trotting writer. I was stunned—well, taken aback anyway, because I had never seen a trotting race. I didn't know the first thing about trotting—racing, yes, but trotting? I had never seen a trotting horse.

I was told I would soon learn, so get started. It didn't take me long to pick it up. After all it was still horse racing, only the horses had a different running action. The first thing I had to learn was to know the difference between a pacer and a trotter. I thought they were all just 'trotters'.

But I soon got to know that a pacer was a horse that moves its two legs on the left side forward simultaneously while the two legs on the right side are going back in unison as well—it's a parallel movement. The trotter, or the Standardbred as it is officially known, has a different action. It moves its legs diagonally, that is, the right front foot moves forward simultaneously with the left rear, then the left front with the right rear.

There was still a lot to learn but I soon picked it up from the friendly trainers and reinsmen involved. I quickly learned that the trotting people were much easier to deal with than the racing people. They were willing to talk about their horses, tell you a story and keep you informed, while the racing people played their cards very close to their chest.

There was one racing trainer who could be downright rude. Pat Quinlan, and he was one of the leading trainers. Not long after I joined *The Argus* racing staff I was told to phone Mr. Quinlan and ask if he had engaged a rider for his horse Peshawar who was down to run on Saturday. The conversation went like this: 'It's Ron Taylor from *The Argus* Mr. Quinlan.' 'Who?' 'Ron Taylor from *The Argus*.' '*The Argus*? I wouldn't wipe my arse on *The Argus*.' Then he hung up. However, he mellowed as time went on, and later, after he had retired, became friendly towards me and would often come up at the races for a chat.

The trotting people though were much more open. Most of the trainers and drivers were country people who had farms or lived off the land and weren't so involved with betting and relying on 'slings' from owners. That's not to say there weren't some big punters—there were, and they gambled heavily.

In the early 1950s there would often be bigger crowds at the night trots at the Showgrounds than there had been at the gallops in the afternoon, and nearly as many bookmakers. But there seemed to be a more homely attitude among the harness racing fraternity, a willingness to help as opposed to keeping you in the dark.

So I enjoyed my stint as a trotting writer. One of the reasons was because it brought me into contact with the members of the racing staff. They were mostly a bit older than me—Jack Elliott, Tom Moon, Jack O'Brien, Percy Cheffers, Wally Willmott, Tom Melross. Bill Condon and Lindsay Mudge. To say they didn't mind a drink, especially Jack and Tom, would be putting it mildly, and I think they thought it their duty to educate me.

You were expected to be a man-about-town, a neat dresser, a hail fellow-well met and a man who could hold his liquor. The liquor you learned from practice. It was common to meet at the races with your colleagues from other papers and have a friendly ale before the first race.

There would be four of five in the school, sometimes more, so a round of drinks would be five or six seven-ounce glasses of beer. Of course you didn't have to complete the shout—as long as you paid your way you could pull out at any time. But we all had a couple of drinks under our belt even before the races started and there was still a whole day to go.

Needless to say there were some hairy rides home from Flemington or Caulfield in Jack's sporty new convertible, but we all survived and were able to tell the tale of Saturday's races in Monday's paper. There were no random breath tests but fortunately for all of us breathalyser testing was introduced in 1976. If you were caught driving with a blood alcohol level of .05 or over you were in trouble—and you still are.

Sometimes I wonder how I survived those early days at *The Argus* and can only attribute my good fortune to meeting, and marrying, Lola, my wife of 49 years.

Ron, 23, joins *The Argus* Newspaper in Melbourne.

10

Married To A Jockey's Daughter

I knew from the moment I met her that Lola was going to be my wife. She was a vivacious person, quick to smile, and someone who would look you in the eye with an openness that invited confidence. Right from the kick-off I wasn't shy with her and felt that if I asked her to share a lemonade with me she would accept. And accept she did.

From there I found out she was a stenographer working with Consolidated Press in Collins Street and that she lived with her parents in Brunswick. She was surprised to learn that I was a racing writer but it did my cause no harm because she informed me her father was an ex-jockey. So right from the start we had common ground.

We had a wonderful life together until she died in 2003. She was such a good person that you would feel like a heel if you did anything to offend her, so I guess that's what has kept me a fairly equitable person throughout my life. Not long after we met I was sent by *The Argus* to cover the Inter-Dominion trotting carnival in Perth in 1953.

When I returned after three weeks away I found that Lola had kept a scrapbook of my reports. So I figured that was a good omen and asked her to marry me. She accepted, thank goodness, but first I had to go through the delicate matter of asking permission of her father. It wasn't as straight forward as you might think.

I got on well with Jim, he being a racing man we spoke the jargon. Jim was a good jockey, perhaps not up there with Frank Dempsey and Billy Duncan who were his contemporaries in the early 1900s, but good enough to be retained by the Sultan of Johore to ride for him in Singapore and Malaysia. When it came to seeking his daughter's hand however, we were on different ground.

Jim didn't doubt that I truly loved Lola but he wanted to know how I was going to keep her. Did I own a house, did I have a car? Was I earning enough for two people to live on, all those sorts of things. Well, no, I didn't have a house, I didn't own a car, but I had a good job and there were prospects of rising up the ladder.

Jim was most concerned that Lola would have a new home to move into after her marriage so he said that if he was to give his permission I would have to start thinking about buying a house. He said that if I could raise the deposit he would guarantee a bank loan for the remainder.

That meant he didn't have to put any money up, but the guarantee was that if I fell short, or couldn't make the repayments, he would be responsible. I told him that was very generous of him and that I wouldn't let him down. That was all he wanted to know so I got his blessing, and after a 12-month engagement, Lola and I were married in July 1954.

But how was I to raise that deposit? There was only one thing for it—give up smoking, drinking and gambling. How hard was that? They were three staples of my life. But I wanted to marry Lola more than anything in my life so, just do it.

After almost a year I had saved enough to put a deposit on a brand new two-bedroom weatherboard house in Ogilvie Street in West Essendon, and we moved in the day we returned from our honeymoon.

We couldn't afford to go to Surfer's Paradise as I would have liked, because we needed furniture for the house and I had to keep on working. So we spent three days at the Grand Hotel in Mildura escaping Melbourne's winter for a brief holiday. Then it was back to work, Lola to her new job as a stenographer for a solicitor in Collins Street, and me to *The Argus*.

Ron and Lola celebrate their engagement.

11

Racing's Golden Era

The 1950s and '60s was a great era for racing. I was lucky enough to see some of the best horses ever to have raced in Australia and to get to know some of the personalities. I was with *The Argus* from 1951 to 1956, a time when Rising Fast was winning all before him, and Tulloch was just beginning his career as a two-year old. They were the two best horses I had seen until Vain came along, then Kingston Town, Black Caviar and Winx.

Many readers may not have seen either Rising Fast or Tulloch, but they were the heroes of their time and captured the public's imagination. I know it can be boring to hear old-timers talk about their favourite horses when you weren't around at the time, but racing is made up of history and to understand it and to love it you have to know something of the great horses of the past.

Of course you can't accurately evaluate horses of different eras, but when you look at what Phar Lap was doing in the early 1930s, and what Winx was doing 80 to 90 years later, you can understand why they are both rated champions of the turf.

I didn't see Phar Lap (my first Melbourne race meeting was 1948 when Rimfire won the Melbourne Cup) but you only have to read what Phar Lap achieved in the spring of 1930 to know that he was one of the greatest horses of all time. I think he is still the greatest. What he did that spring will never be repeated. No horse in the world these days would be asked to run four times in eight days over varying distances from 1600 metres to 3600 metres. It wouldn't even be contemplated.

But that's what trainer Harry Telford asked of Phar Lap and the big chestnut, dubbed the 'Red Terror' didn't let him down. Starting with the Melbourne Stakes (later the LKS McKinnon Stakes) over 2000 metres on Saturday 1 November, Phar Lap won by three lengths starting at 5/1 on.

On the Tuesday, he came out in the Melbourne Cup, 3200 metres, with 9 stone 12 lb (62.5kg) on his back and won, seemingly effortlessly, by three lengths starting at 11/8 on, the shortest priced favourite in the history of the great race.

Then on the Thursday, Telford took him back to 1600 meters in the Linlithgow Stakes and Phar Lap, again starting at 7/1 on, played with the opposition to win by four lengths from Mollison, who was one of Australia's best sprinters.

As if that wasn't enough Telford started him again the following Saturday in the C.B. Fisher Plate over 2400 metres. There wasn't a horse in Australia who could hold a candle to Phar Lap and only two lined up against him, Second Wind, who had finished second to him in the Melbourne Cup, and Lineage.

Such was Phar Lap's dominance the bookies didn't even bother to bet on the race, so no starting price was recorded against Phar Lap's three and a half lengths victory over Second Wind. That was the end of Phar Lap's spring campaign, the most remarkable four days in racing's long history.

I've detailed those wins by Phar Lap so that you can put him into perspective with Rising Fast, the best horse in Australia in the early 1950s, and the best horse I had seen until Tulloch came along shortly afterwards.

I won't attempt to compare Rising Fast with Carbine

because they raced so many years apart—64 years between their Melbourne Cup wins—but I mention Carbine because there are some historians who rate him a better horse than Phar Lap.

Carbine had an extraordinary autumn in 1890 when he won five races at Randwick in eight days. First of all he took out the Autumn Stakes, 1½ miles, on 5 April then two days later won the Sydney Cup two miles carrying 61.25kg.

Three days later he won the All-Aged Stakes, one mile, then four races later on the *same day* saddled up again to win the Cumberland Stakes, two miles. His fifth win came the following two days in the Cumberland Plate over three miles to complete an amazing sequence.

Later the same year Carbine won the Melbourne Cup in record time carrying 66kg, the highest weight ever for a winner, and he defeated 38 rivals, the biggest field ever. So there is ample justification for comparing him with Phar Lap, and, for some, even to put him ahead. But in the hearts of the majority of racegoers I believe Phar Lap will always be No 1.

Not only was he a champion racehorse he was a national idol. His fame was so great that after he won the world's richest race at that time, the Agua Caliente Handicap in New Mexico, his connections even received a congratulatory telegram from King George V of England.

If you haven't seen film of Phar Lap winning in New Mexico you should go to YouTube and watch his amazing performance. He did it with a bloodied heel, beating the best horses in America and running a race record. His fame at the time was so great that the wags were saying that if Phar Lap could stand on his hind legs and talk he would be the prime minister.

The Agua Caliente Handicap however was Phar Lap's only start in America, in fact it was his last race. A few weeks later he was dead. His death shocked the racing world and there were several theories as to what caused it, including being poisoned by gangsters. The *Truth* of it was that he died of a severe attack of arsenic poisoning brought on by years of being fed small doses of Fowler's Solution, an arsenic-based tonic.

There has always been conjecture as to what caused Phar Lap's death but in 2008 the Melbourne Museum released the findings of a forensic investigation by Ivan Kempson and David Henry. They had been able to secure hairs from Phar Lap's mane taken from his mounted hide which was on exhibition in the Museum. Their examination confirmed the presence of arsenic.

12

The Pyjama Girl Mystery

Although I never saw Phar Lap race he has always been my hero, right from the time I first saw his enormous heart displayed at the Institute of Anatomy in Canberra. I was 12 and had just started at Canberra High, which was just across the road from the Institute of Anatomy (now the National Film and Sound Archive building).

To fill in lunch hour I would walk across to the Institute to look at the various exhibits. It was rumoured around the school that the body of the murdered 'Pyjama Girl' was stored there, in the basement, in a bath of formalin to preserve it.

I digress here but the story is worth telling because it was such big news right around Australia, sometimes even knocking World War II off the front pages. The victim was an attractive 23-year-old unidentified woman. Her body was found hidden in a culvert under a back road near Albury in 1934, so badly burned that it could not be recognised.

Police put the body on display at the morgue in Albury and the public was invited to inspect it in the hope someone would recognise her. After a time, when no positive identification had been made, the body was transferred to the Sydney University.

But somewhere between Albury and Sydney I believe the Pyjama Girl, so named because she was wearing yellow pyjamas when discovered, spent some time in Canberra. Otherwise why would a group of young school kids looking for adventure go scooting across to the Institute of Anatomy to see the body of a naked woman if, in fact, she wasn't there?

We never found her though, despite looking into every corner of the building. But I do recall that down a flight of stairs was a door that was always locked. That's where we reckoned she was held. Well, that's my story anyway. But official records make no mention of it.

Eventually, 10 years after the body was discovered, a Melbourne man, Antonio Agostini came forward and confessed. The woman was his wife. Agostini, was sentenced to six years jail for manslaughter and after serving three years was deported to Italy.

I mention the Pyjama Girl as an aside because it was a story that captured the imagination of the public. But the real reason for me visiting the Institute so often was to see Phar Lap's heart. It intrigued me because of its size compared with that of an Army remount horse which was displayed alongside it.

Both hearts were stored in glass cases of formalin, a solution used for preserving scientific specimens. Phar Lap's heart weighed 6.35kg and was twice the size of the remount horse which weighed between 3-4kg. That weight is generally accepted as the weight of the heart of an average-sized horse, so why was Phar Lap's heart so big? Did it explain why he was such a superior racehorse?

I was intrigued, but I was only a young kid and horse racing wasn't one on my priorities. Canberra wasn't a racing town by any means. There was a racecourse, Acton, and one or two local trainers, but the raceday programme was made up of participants from all over southern New South Wales, places like Wagga

Wagga, Yass, Goulburn, Crookwell, Braidwood, Bungendore, Queanbeyan, Cooma and others.

As a schoolboy, my sporting interests were with football and cricket. Racing came later. It wasn't until I watched a television documentary many years afterwards, in 2009 I think it was, that I began to think seriously about Phar Lap again. This was a television 'expose' compiled by Channel 9 investigative reporter Ian Leslie into the cause of Phar Lap's death.

A mock trial was set up with Tommy Woodcock, Phar Lap's trainer in the dock accused of killing the champion. Various people gave 'evidence' of how they saw Tommy feeding Phar Lap a white powder alleged to contain arsenic. I was a great admirer of Tommy, he was one of the nicest gentlemen you would ever meet, so I was disappointed to see how he was portrayed.

To be honest I couldn't tell what was fact and what was fiction from all the various interviews with people who said they knew Tommy. One of the statements in particular bowled me over. It was said that the heart of Phar Lap that was on show in Canberra was not that of Phar Lap at all. It belonged to a draught horse!

This was a great blow to me, who, as a schoolkid had spent hours admiring that heart at the Institute of Anatomy. I couldn't believe that wasn't really Phar Lap's heart so I did some investigating of my own. I discovered that as soon as reports of Phar Lap's death reached Australia, veterinarian Dr. Stewart McKay of the Sydney University cabled the horse's owner, David Davis, in America asking for Phar Lap's heart. He wanted to preserve it as an interesting relic for the future study of racehorse development.

Davis, who had previously leased half of Phar Lap to his trainer Harry Telford, immediately got in touch with his vet William Neilsen, who did the first post mortem on Phar Lap, instructing him to preserve the heart. This was done and the heart was shipped back to Australia accompanied by Phar Lap's jockey Billy Elliot.

After it had been examined by Dr. McKay and his associate, Professor Welsh, at Sydney University it was forwarded to the Institute of Anatomy in Canberra at the request of Harry Telford. The veterinarians had removed a section of the heart to measure the thickness of the wall and that is why when you see Phar Lap's heart it has a gap in it.

The story of the heart belonging to a draught horse was apparently inspired by a report that two such horses had died in paddock near where Phar Lap was stabled. Autopsies had been carried out on them with the heart of one, allegedly, being substituted for Phar Lap's.

Just for comparison I made inquiries at knackeries and abattoirs to see if someone could show me a draught horse's heart. No one could.

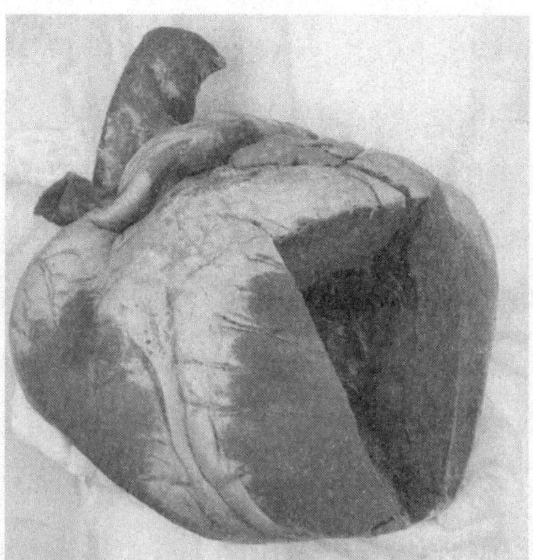

Phar Lap's heart. Note the piece cut out to show the thickness of the wall.

13

Rising Fast Was One Of The Greatest

I think it fair to say that Phar Lap will always be remembered as the greatest horse ever to have raced in Australia. It isn't just because of his ability on the track but because of the inspiration he provided at a dark time in Australia's history, the Great Depression years, when his memorable victories lifted the spirits of the nation.

He was a national hero and his sudden death in America, when at the peak of his career, only added to the legend he had already created. Some people will say that Carbine and Winx have greater claims to fame, and, judged on their performances, that's understandable. Their contribution will always be an extremely prominent part of our racing history.

But when you are comparing them with Phar Lap we are dealing with different eras, and therefore there can never be a really definitive answer to the question of which horse was the greatest.

To rationalise Carbine's contribution you have to go back 160 years so his career is not really relevant to what I am writing about today. Racing has undergone revolutionary changes in terms of breeding, training, drug control and track management to name a few. But no story about racing in Australia can ever be complete without acknowledging that Carbine and Winx deserve to be rated immortals.

I can write with some authority only about horses I have seen, so that's why Rising Fast is also prominent in these discussions. But, before I remind you what he achieved, let me tell of the encounter I had with his trainer and a ferocious Alsatian dog.

Victorians at first didn't know a lot about Rising Fast who had won a few Hack races in New Zealand. They were called Hack races but they were not for 'hacks' in the common sense of that term. They were similar to what we in Australia would call 'restricted' races But Rising Fast had also won a weight-for-age race at Paeroa which gave his owner, Mr. Lester Spring, and his trainer Ivan Tucker the confidence to take him to Australia.

It was 1954 and Rising Fast began his campaign at the Brisbane winter carnival to warm him up for the Melbourne spring. I began to take notice of the horse after he ran third in the Doomben Cup and followed that up with a win at weight-for-age in the James Barnes Stakes. I was still working for *The Argus* and when Ivan Tucker brought him to Melbourne I thought he would make good material for a story.

Tucker had rented a property in Edinburgh Street, Flemington, so I rang the stables in the hope of speaking to him. No answer. I needed a story for the next day's paper and Rising Fast was my best option. So it was imperative I speak to his trainer. The only thing to do was to go to the stables and see Tucker in person.

I drove out to Flemington, found the house and knocked on the front door. No answer. Undaunted I tried the back entrance. It was a barred by a high gate so I tried knocking on it. This brought no response either but I knew someone was there because I could hear horses clip-clopping behind it.

There was only one thing for it. I was tall enough to grasp the top of the gate so I hauled myself up and jumped down the other side—only to be met by the gaping jaws of an Alsatian dog who was straining on the end of his chain. The commotion brought a quick response, as a short wiry man emerged from one of the boxes and said 'What the devil are you doing?', or words to that effect.

I assumed this to be Mr. Tucker, who I knew was an ex-jockey, so I gave him my name and explained I was from *The Argus* and had jumped the fence because I couldn't make anyone hear at the house. He said: 'Lucky for you the dog was on a chain, we let him run loose at night to keep out any intruders.'

Fortunately for me Ivan Tucker turned out to be a decent fellow and gave me an outline of what Rising Fast's program would be in Melbourne. So I got my story, but I never tried those tactics again.

Rising Fast had an incredible spring in 1954 winning in succession the Turnbull Stakes, the Caulfield Stakes, Caulfield Cup, W.S. Cox Plate, L.K.S. Mackinnon Stakes, Melbourne Cup and the C.B. Fisher Plate. Until Might and Power came along in 1997 he was the only horse to have won the Caulfield Cup, Cox Plate and Melbourne Cup in the same year.

The following season Rising Fast won the Caulfield Cup again and was primed to make history in the Melbourne Cup. No horse had ever won the Caulfield Cup-Melbourne Cup double two years running and, with an ounce of luck, he would have done it.

He was thwarted however by the lightweight Toparoa who carried 7 stone 8lb (48kg) to Rising Fast's 10 stone (63.5kg). His defeat caused great controversy and arguments still exist today that he should have been declared the winner.

The discussion centred around the decision of the stewards to suspend Toparoa's rider Neville Sellwood for two months for causing interference to Rising Fast in the straight. Toparoa had drifted out on Rising Fast coming to the winning post taking him wider out on the track before going on to win by three-quarters of a length.

Many spectators expected Rising Fast's jockey Bill Williamson to lodge a protest, but none was forthcoming. What everyone wanted to know afterwards was: if the interference was so severe as to warrant such a long suspension, why didn't the stewards lodge a protest of their own?

Well firstly, the Chief Steward, Mr. E.S.A. Bell, didn't believe the interference made the difference between winning and losing for Rising Fast. Also he was annoyed that despite his pre-race address to the jockeys that he wanted the Cup to be cleanly run it was one of the worst on record for interference. So when Sellwood allowed Toparoa to drift out on Rising Fast he bore the full brunt of Mr. Bell's ire.

The story doesn't end there and I'll go into it a little further along in this book when I tell you about a friend of mine, Ted Humphries, who backed Rising Fast to win both Cups for 250,000 pounds. Imagine what that would be worth today! But right now I want to continue with those great horses of the past so that you can get the modern champions into perspective.

People say you can't compare horses of different eras, and that's right if you take an era to be marking the beginning of a new and distinct period of time. But there were only 40 years between Carbine and Phar Lap and even less between Phar Lap and Rising Fast, so I would hardly call that an 'era'.

And, even though there is more than 60 years between Rising Fast and Winx, I think they still ran under relatively the same conditions. So a comparison between Rising Fast and Winx is not unrealistic.

You might think that the times the horses ran would give you a good indication of their ability, but the distance of races has varied so much over the years that you can't rely on times. For instance the W.S. Cox Plate, which both Rising Fast and Winx (four times) have won, has been run over several distances since it was first run in 1922. It was run over 9 ½ furlongs when Phar Lap won in 1930 and over 1 ¼ miles when Rising Fast won in 1954, so you can't get a comparison there.

Winx is listed as the record holder for the Cox Plate winning in a time of 2.02.94 in 2017, but Better Loosen Up won in 2.01.5 in 1990 and that is also listed as a record. Both races are recorded as being run over 2040 metres so it's useless trying to compare horses on times from old records. The explanation for them both being credited as record-holders is that they ran on different surfaces. In 1995 Moonee Valley dug up its grass track and replaced it with an all-weather StrathAyr surface which is comprised of a mixture of turf and sand. There is a time differential between the two surfaces hence the need for new records to be recognised.

When Melbourne went metric in 1972 the distance of the W.S. Cox Plate changed to 2050 metres and was changed again in 1986 to 2040 metres, the distance it is today. Anyway, it's all in the eye of the beholder and everyone is entitled to their opinion.

For what it's worth I think Winx would have beaten Rising Fast had they met in a W.S. Cox Plate, simply because she was the more brilliant of the two. Comparing the two horses I can rely on what I have seen. I have a distinct memory of Rising Fast, how his coat dappled and gleamed when the sun shone on it, and how regally he carried his tall and powerful frame.

Rising Fast was at his best at distances of a mile and beyond, particularly at one and a half miles. Winx on the other hand was just as effective at 1400 metres as at 2040 metres. She virtually was never tried beyond that distance although she did win the Queensland Oaks over 2200 metres and ran second in the

Australian Oaks over 2400 metres. But those races were as a three-year-old and her connections didn't see any merit in pursuing a staying program.

Two of the best horses I have seen in more than 70 years of going racing were Vain and Black Caviar. Both were champions and their deeds have sparked many arguments as to which was the better sprinter. For what it's worth I'll give you my impression.

14

Vain v Black Caviar

There is a mountain of public opinion that says Black Caviar is the best sprinter Australia has seen. Of course there is, because she was unbeaten in 25 starts and went to England and beat the best they had to offer over there. But for sheer speed my vote still goes to Vain.

I saw a lot of Vain and wrote many stories about him in *Truth*. He was just such a sensational horse that's why I have such a strong memory of his performances. He was a magnificent colt to look at. Not tall, not short, just beautifully balanced. You could call him stocky, or chunky but those words don't quite hit the mark. They don't encompass how elegant he was as well, or reflect his short cannons and robust hindquarters, the hallmarks of a sprinter. You only had to look at him to see he was a class racehorse.

Vain's main attribute was that he would hit the ground running. He would be lengths in front of his rivals before they even realised the race was on. The Craven A Stakes, run at Flemington on Derby Day in 1969 was a case in point. The race was an open handicap over six furlongs up the straight and Vain was carrying 8 stone 7lb (54kg), five pounds above weight-for-age, a weight record for a three-year-old at the time.

Vain, as usual, was first out of the gates and before you

could blink he was two lengths in front. From then on it was just a procession. He just kept getting further ahead until he was 12 lengths in front at the winning post. I can't recall a longer winning margin in a big sprint.

Black Caviar's biggest winning margin was six lengths in the Schweppes Stakes, 1200 metres, at Moonee Valley in 2011 but she was hard held going to the post and could have won by much more. It's difficult to say what her greatest winning margin could have been because she was rarely ridden out. That's what makes it so difficult to get a true comparison between Vain and Black Caviar, because the mare was so rarely let go.

Winx, another great champion, was also capable of winning by a space. Her longest winning margin was 7.3 lengths in George Ryder Stakes,1500m, at Rosehill in March 2017, but she was ridden out to the line. Anyway it's not fair to compare Winx with Vain and Black Caviar as they were essentially sprinters whereas Winx excelled at 2000 metres, notably by winning four W.S. Cox Plates over the 2040-metre journey.

But back to Vain and that memorable Cup Week of 1969. After bolting in with the Craven A Stakes on the Saturday—his jockey, Pat Hyland, described it as 'an exercise gallop'—he came out on the Thursday and gave a scintillating exhibition of sustained speed to win the Linlithgow Stakes by six lengths and run a Flemington record of 1 minute 23 seconds for the seven furlongs (1400m).

Vain pulled up so well and fresh that trainer Jim Moloney decided he should attempt the grand slam by tackling the George Adams Handicap (1 mile) two days later on the Saturday. It was again a case of 'shut the gate'. Vain led all the way to win by 1¼ lengths from Our Faith. What made the run so meritorious was that Vain carried 55.5kg which represented 4.5kg above weight-for-age, a record for a three-year-old.

Vain won 10 of his 12 starts so there are several more races I could describe, all pointing to what a great racehorse he was. I'll mention just two of them, the Golden Slipper Stakes and the Champagne Stakes of 1969. In the Golden Slipper he was up against Sydney's champion two-year-old Special Girl, rated by the locals as unbeatable.

Special Girl had won her first two starts, each by 10 lengths, starting at 14/1 on. She went into the Slipper with one more run, a win at 10/1 on in the Widden Stakes. She won by only three-quarters of a length from Celina but her jockey George Moore had eased her down, earning a reprimand from the stewards. Moore declared Special Girl the fastest two-year-old he had ever ridden, an opinion that ensured the filly started a hot favourite at 13/8 on in the Slipper with Vain at 4/1.

But it was 'no race'. Vain burst from the gates like a rocket and was never headed. He won by four lengths. Special Girl couldn't get near him and finished fifth.

The Champagne Stakes was run a week after Vain was surprisingly beaten at 6/1 on in the AJC Sires' Produce Stakes by Beau Babylon, a 33/1 chance. It had been a wet week in Sydney and Vain had missed a gallop when the grass tracks were closed on the Tuesday prior to the race. Come race day Vain led as usual but knocked up and was beaten three-quarters of a length by the fast finishing Beau Babylon.

It was a different story the following Saturday in the Champagne Stakes. The rain had gone, the tracks had dried out, and Vain was fitter. Favourite at 11/8 on Vain was quickly into his role as pacemaker and the further they went the further he went ahead. He just romped in by 10 lengths and ran an Australian record for a two-year-old clocking 1 minute 9.2 for the six furlongs. He broke the previous record held by Pago Pago by more than half a second.

Vain would not only leave the barrier like a bullet. he could keep going. For instance he won the Maribyrnong Plate as a two-year-old by eight lengths and the following season won the Craven A Stakes, six furlongs, up the Flemington straight by 12 lengths. At the time, in 1970, it was the longest winning margin recorded in a major sprint in Australia, and I don't recall it being beaten since. That was the difference between Vain and Black Caviar. He just jumped and ran and he didn't stop running.

Black Caviar, on the other hand, won most of her races hard held. Rarely did her rider Luke Nolen let her run right out to the winning post. She always seemed to be loafing alongside her rivals and when Nolen did give her more rein he only let her do enough to win. But there were two or three occasions when she really had to pull out all stops and they were the races that really stamped her as a true champion.

One of those occasions was the T.J. Smith Stakes at Randwick in 2011 when she was challenged by Hay List, who was 'flying' at the time. Coming over the rise about 400 metres from home Hay List was four lengths in front of Black Caviar and Nolen had to get busy on the mare and ride her hard to go after him. It was one of the few times Black Caviar was put under pressure. But she responded brilliantly and quickly reined Hay List in to win by four lengths.

The other occasion was the Diamond Jubilee Stakes at Royal Ascot when Nolen had to pull the whip passing the 400 metres to keep her mind on the job. Close to the post Nolen, believing he had it won, eased up and so did Black Caviar. It was almost a fatal mistake. Fortunately there was just time for Nolen to realise his error and get her going again to win by a head.

So there you have it, two great champions—Black Caviar unbeaten in 25 starts, Vain winner of 10 from 12 attempts. From a statistical standpoint Black Caviar holds sway over Vain, but to my eye if you put both horses down over 1200 metres at Flemington at weight-for-age Vain would win. Simply because he would get so far in front she couldn't catch him. It would be close, no doubt. That's my opinion, but who really knows?

HORSE OF THE YEAR

VAIN (Ch. colt 3 yrs. Wilkes°—Elated) is judged by Bred To Win as Horse of the Year in Australia for the racing season ended July 31, 1970.

15

Tulloch Was A True Champion

Then there was Tulloch, Australia's champion three-year-old in 1957. Tulloch deserves a chapter all to himself because although it is more than 60 years since his electrifying win in the '57 Caulfield Cup, I still regard him as the best horse I have seen, even after seeing Winx win four W.S. Cox Plates.

Which is the better of the two horses? How do I really know? How could you tell unless you put them both in the same race over 2000 metres and let them fight it out? But that can never happen. So it's just one man's opinion against another's.

But it is fair to say that Winx is the best horse we have seen in Australia since Tulloch. And that period includes Kingston Town, who won three W.S. Cox Plates compared to Winx's record-breaking four.

Winx captured the imagination of the public and instilled admiration for her brilliant racing style, which enabled her to win 37 races, 33 in succession, and 25 at Group One level.

Why then was Tulloch so special? To me, it isn't just the races he won, and how he won them, but the way he captured the attention of people who weren't what you would call 'racing followers'.

Australians love sporting champions, whatever they are, animal or human. We promoted Cathy Freeman to hero status when she won an Olympic Gold Medal and declared Black Caviar a legend after she strung together 25 successive victories.

And, more recently, there is Winx. Everyone knows Winx, you don't have to be a racing fanatic to know that she was a champion racehorse. She figured in the national news bulletins whenever she won a race, or even if there was a hiccup in her racing preparation. Her health and well-being was documented almost daily in the newspapers so she became the talk of the town for the general public not just racing followers. That's the mark of a true champion—like Tulloch.

The discussion over whether Tulloch should run in the 1957 Melbourne Cup as a three-year-old sparked arguments all over the country. The newspapers were full of it, the owner at odds with his trainer.

To put it in a nutshell Tulloch's owner, Mr. E.A. Haley, believed that the two miles of the Melbourne Cup was too taxing for a young horse. His concern was for the welfare of his horse. The trainer, Tommy Smith, believed it was just a matter of Tulloch lining up for him to win. Smith was Australia's leading trainer and nobody would dispute his ability to know what a racehorse might be capable of.

The arguments for and against raged until in the end it was driving Smith so mad he threw his hands up and gave in. The tragedy of that decision was that Tulloch would have bolted in with that Melbourne Cup. How do we know? Well, look at it this way. On the Saturday before the Melbourne Cup Tulloch, starting at 10/1 on, won the Victoria Derby by eight lengths from Prince Darius.

Three days later Prince Darius ran second in the Cup beaten a neck by Straight Draw. So by how far would Tulloch have won?

But the mark of a true champion isn't just judged by the

races it has won. It's the effect the horse has on those watching that also counts. And Tulloch certainly stirred emotions. I'll never forget the day he won the Queen's Plate (1 1/4m) at Flemington at his first start for 23 months, following an illness that almost killed him.

Tulloch was at death's door for months as his trainer, veterinary surgeons and well-wishers tried every remedy known to man to cure him. It was a debilitating illness that left him so weak he was hardly able to stand on his feet.

Finally the breakthrough came one morning when Percy Sykes, the vet who was his constant attendant, went into his stall and was almost knocked down as Tulloch rushed at him. 'He's back' exclaimed Percy under his breath as Tulloch's fiery temperament reasserted itself. And back he was—Percy's remedies had finally worked.

Smith chose the Queen's Plate on 12 March 1960 for Tulloch's return. It was an ambitious choice because the distance was one and a quarter miles, and no one in Australia at that time ever dreamed of running a horse first up over such a journey, particularly after so long a break. It was the Race of the Century. Well, it was to that time. We hadn't heard of Bonecrusher and Our Waverley Star's epic Cox Plate battle then.

Only five horses lined up for the race and two of them were stars, Tulloch and Lord. Another was Mac, who had won the Adelaide Cup the year before. Despite Tulloch's great reputation hard-nosed punters looked past him as the likely winner. They made the in-form horse Lord favourite at 9/4, Mac was 11/4 and Tulloch started at 4/1.

I was willing for Tulloch to win but knew it wasn't going to be easy. Lord was a crack weight-for-age horse and he was flying having beaten the brilliant Noholme in the St. George Stakes at his previous start. Geoff Lane on Lord dictated the pace of the race with Neville Sellwood on Tulloch content to sit back on him and have the last run.

Tulloch joined Lord at the top of the straight and the two settled down to fight it out. For the last two furlongs they went head and head. The crowd was delirious with excitement. They were still locked together at the post and the Judge had to call for the photo.

When Tulloch's number went up there were wild scenes of elation. I was watching from the Press Box below the Hill Stand and had a great view of the lawns where the public was congregated. You've read about men throwing their hats in the air in their excitement, well it was true that day. Hats were flying everywhere.

Someone in the crowd called: 'Three cheers for Tulloch'. It caught on immediately and was taken up all around the course, on the lawns and in the grandstands. When they had finished one chorus they took it up again and 'Three Cheers' rang out a second time.

I've never heard anything like that since, not even for Black Caviar or Winx. At the winner's stall Tommy Smith was overcome and well-wishers came from everywhere to embrace him. But the man really responsible for getting Tulloch to the post that day was nowhere to be seen. Sykes, the vet, was hiding behind the grandstand crying his eyes out. How do I know? Because Percy himself told me.

'It was the only time in my life that I cried,' he said. 'I thought Tulloch had been beaten. Someone came up to me and said "Bad luck". It did look as though Tulloch had been beaten. Then when the number went up there were all those hats in the air, I felt tears running down my cheeks. I couldn't stop them. So I went to the back of the stand to get away from everybody.'

Now that Tulloch was back in form he continued on his merry way. Tommy took him back to Sydney and three weeks after his Melbourne success Tulloch won the Chipping Norton Stakes at Warwick Farm. He won three more races in quick succession before Tommy put him away for the winter. It was time to plan ahead for the 1960 Centenary Melbourne Cup. Tulloch was allotted 10.1. Only two horses, Carbine,10.5 in 1890 and Archer, 10.2 (1862), had won with more weight.

16

Neville Sellwood Controversy

The 1960 Centenary Melbourne Cup was one of the most talked about races of all time, and it's still going on today. You would not believe how many versions I have heard how Neville Sellwood, Tulloch's jockey, pulled him up. Tulloch, starting 3/1 favourite, finished seventh, four lengths behind the winner, Hi Jinx. Of course there is always talk when a Melbourne Cup favourite is beaten. I couldn't count the number of times I have heard that the jockey 'pulled it up'. They said that about Sellwood too, but in all the history of the Melbourne Cup no jockey has been found guilty of that offence.

There was some justification however for punters having Sellwood in the gun. He did set the horse an enormous task. Six furlongs from home Tulloch was running 26th in a field of 31. Dow Street had fallen otherwise there would have been 32 runners at that point. Tulloch was giving the leaders 50 lengths start. The general opinion was that he was never going to win from there—and he didn't. But he made an extraordinary effort to be beaten only four lengths.

Could Tulloch have won had he been closer in the run? You could be excused for thinking so, but it doesn't automatically apply. I'll never forget the New Zealander, Kiwi, winning the 1983 Melbourne Cup coming from 30, or more, lengths behind, second last in a strung out field of 24 with 1000 metres to go.

I had tipped Kiwi to win in *Truth*'s Special Melbourne Cup edition under the blazing headline 'Kiwi to Shine'. The caption underneath read: *KIWI will polish off his rivals in the $310,000 Melbourne Cup on Tuesday—and make history by becoming the first horse to win without a warm-up race in Australia.*

When I saw him so far back I thought to myself *what an idiot* I was to tip a horse I knew so little about. Kiwi had arrived in Australia only on the Thursday before the Cup and the public really had only the form guide, showing his New Zealand runs, to go on. That's why he started at 9/1. But I did have some good information.

My friend David Coles, who owned the Coles Bloodstock Agency, had seen Kiwi win the Wellington Cup over 3200 metres at Trentham back in January and he told me he thought the horse was a good thing. My former boss Jack Elliott had also seen that Wellington Cup and he too tipped Kiwi. But we were the only two out of more than 20 Melbourne newspaper tipsters to do so.

Nevertheless, at the 1000 metre mark I was kicking myself for being so stupid. I thought there was no way he could win from so far back. But his jockey Jimmy Cassidy stirred Kiwi up and the horse began to surge forward. Cassidy saved ground, somehow weaving him through a pack of horses until he was able to get to the outside with little more than 100 metres to run.

From that point Kiwi sprouted wings and won by one and three quarter lengths from Noble Comment and Mr. Jazz. I couldn't believe it. That race however taught me a lesson—never write off a horse because you think they are giving an impossible start. Many have done it. Think of Bernborough, Rough Habit, Chautaqua and the Hong Kong marvel, Pakistan Star.

So despite all the stories and opinions to the contrary, I can't condemn Sellwood. Sure, I couldn't understand his tactics, but he was a world class jockey riding in Australia's richest and most sought after race. He always said he rode the horse to give it it's best chance to win.

I often wondered after reading all the reports on the race, and the level of criticism of Sellwood's ride, why I never saw reference to it in a steward's inquiry. The answer is: there was no inquiry.

I didn't become aware of this until nearly 20 years later when I was invited to watch the official film of the 1960 Cup with the then Chief Stipendiary Steward, Mr. Jim Ahern, and former champion jockey Jack Purtell who had become a steward. Mr. Ahern was also a member of the stewards panel, chaired by Mr. Alan Bell, back in 1960 which saw Hi Jinx win the Cup from Howsie and Illumquh. Tulloch was seventh.

Mr. Ahern told me that the film we were watching confirmed his opinion at the time that Tulloch had been given every chance to win. 'Under his big weight (10 st. 1lb) he could not go the early pace,' Mr. Ahern said. 'Sellwood wisely let him become balanced. To have forced him early would have been suicidal. Yet he had him close enough when racing with Illumquh, to win, had he been able to accelerate in his usual manner.'

Sellwood's words when he dismounted bore out Mr. Ahern's opinion. 'The weight beat him.' Sellwood said. 'He was lacking dash from the six furlongs to the turn. At one stage I was trailing Ilumquh and Howsie, but Tulloch couldn't go with them when they accelerated.'

Did Sellwood overdo the waiting tactics? We'll never know. But what we do know is that defeat did not tarnish Tulloch's image one iota. Four days after the Cup Tulloch bolted in the with the C.B. Fisher Plate.

Tommy Smith couldn't believe he was beaten in the Cup. During one of our many conversations about the race he told me: 'I've never in my life seen a horse ridden so badly. They (the stewards) didn't have him up that day. I thought they'd have him up for sure.

'He was sitting on him. He only rode him from the turn home. But he finished seventh, and he didn't ride him out. I've never seen anything like it in my life. He said to me "He couldn't go?" At his next start he won by 10 lengths (actually it was five lengths).

'But you can't get anything back. What's the good of squealing. That's the punt.'

Otherwise, the controversy over Sellwood's ride was only in the minds of the public and the commentators. The stewards had no problem with it. And that's the key to it really. The steward in charge Alan Bell, had a reputation of being the strictest steward in Australia. The jockeys feared him and trembled when called before him.

But he had a softer side too. When champion jockey Harry White was an apprentice he was never out of trouble. After a string of suspensions that threatened to end his career Alan Bell invited him to his home for a private chat.

Harry told me that Mr. Bell had told him what he had to do overcome his bad habits. Causing interference was only one of them, drinking and lairising were also high on Harry's agenda. So Harry got the message, reformed himself and went on to win four Melbourne Cups, becoming one of Australia's best-known riders.

After the Melbourne Cup Tulloch was spelled and came back the following autumn to win five of his 11 starts, going out in a blaze of glory winning the Brisbane Cup, carrying 9 stone 12lb. (62.5kg). In all his 53 starts he was only ever unplaced once—that Melbourne Cup.

So while Tommy missed out on the 1960 Melbourne Cup he did manage to win the race twice, with Toparoa—ridden by

Sellwood—in 1955 and Just A Dash (P. Cook) in 1981. However, he told me he should have won the race eight times. I'll tell you more about that when I give you my personal insight into Tommy later on.

17

The Penetrometer

I have often been asked 'What was your greatest day at the races?' My first thought was the day Tulloch came back after almost two years off the track and won The Queen's Plate, 1¼ miles, at Flemington. I'll never forget it because of the titanic battle he had with Lord. They went head and head for two furlongs before Tulloch nosed in front right on the post to win by a short half-head.

The crowd went wild. Someone called 'three cheers for Tulloch' The cry was picked up around the course and Flemington rocked. And when the first chorus was finished the crowd gave another 'three cheers' for an encore. I have never heard anything like it since.

Except, perhaps, for the roar that greeted Winx when she loomed up on the home turn to join the leaders in her third W.S. Cox Plate. Everyone knew that she was going to win from there and the 50,000 people at Moonee Valley roared in unison to create a cacophony that made your hair stand up.

But was that my *greatest* day at the races? It was certainly one of the most memorable, but the *greatest* doesn't necessarily refer to a horse race. There are two *great* days I had at the races that didn't involve a particular horse, or a particular race, or a particular bet. One was at the premier French racecourse

Longchamp, and the other was at the now underwater Acton racecourse in Canberra.

Let me tell you about the Longchamp experience first. It is most significant because it resulted in the Penetrometer being introduced to Victoria.

It was my good fortune back in the 1970s and 80s to take racing tours around the world to see all the big races. This often included the French Derby in Paris, and, before we set off, I would write to the President of the French Jockey Club, Jean Romanet, asking if he could set aside reserved seats in the Grandstand for our group. He was always obliging and we developed a good friendship.

One year he said to me: 'Why don't you come back with your wife when you are not taking a tour? I will have more time to entertain you.' I took him at his word and in 1984 Lola and I set off for a holiday in Europe, notifying M. Romanet when we would be in Paris.

You can imagine my surprise when we landed at Charles De Gaulle Airport to find a uniformed chauffeur in the luggage collection area holding up a sign that read 'Mr. Ron Taylor'. A quick chat revealed that he had been sent by M. Romanet to drive us to our hotel and to advise us of arrangements to have lunch at Longchamp on Sunday.

Duly on Sunday the chauffeur was back again to drive us to the racecourse where we met Jean Romanet in the Grand Dining Room. I don't remember what we ate, but I do remember what we drank—two bottles of Pouilly-Fuisse (chardonnay) so it was a convivial meal. The conversation was interrupted by an announcement over the course broadcast that the going had been rated as 'good'. This prompted me to ask how they calculated the state of the track in Paris. M. Romanet explained they were guided by an implement called a Penetrometer.

I had never heard of a penetrometer. Certainly I could not recall having heard the word used in Australia. M. Romanet told me the French punters took the state of the going very seriously and said the old-fashioned method of testing the ground with the heel of a shoe, or a pencil, had gone out with button up boots.

M. Romanet explained that the penetrometer was a steel rod, a little over a metre in length, which had a weight of a kilo at the top. By pulling a trigger the weight would drop a full metre down a shaft connecting with a one-centimetre square which it would push into the ground. How far the rod went in depended on the softness or hardness of the track.

This procedure was repeated every 200 metres right around the track, first a metre out from the running rail then again two metres out. The depth the rod went into the soil was recorded in centimetres and then averaged out.

I won't go any further into the technicalities of it all as it takes too long to explain, and you would only get bored trying to make head and tail out of it. But I did go into some more detail in an article I wrote for *Truth* when I returned to Australia.

This caught the eye of the track manager at Sandown racecourse for the VATC (now Melbourne Racing Club) Mr. Brian Green, who then contacted M. Romanet asking for a penetrometer device to be sent out to him. This was done and Mr. Green experimented with it before recommending its use.

So that's how the penetrometer came into being in Victoria.

But what I didn't know was that the penetrometer had been in use in Sydney, at Rosehill and Canterbury race tracks, for several years. As I said earlier I had never heard of it, and I wasn't aware of any Melbourne people knowing about it either. But if it was being used in Sydney why wasn't it adopted in Melbourne years before?

I can only think it was complacency on behalf of the Melbourne clubs. They obviously didn't think it was necessary.

After my penetrometer story in *Truth* was published, I was soon brought up to speed on the issue by the Racecourse Manager for the Sydney Turf Cub, Mr. John Jeffs, who wrote me a letter dated 20 July 1984, letting me know that he had been using the penetrometer since 1976.

He told me that by using this device he had been able to estimate times for races run at Rosehill and Canterbury to within three to four tenths of a second, regardless of track conditions or weather. So, by comparing previous readings, if he got a penetrometer reading of, say, 2.31 he could equate that to a time of 1.12 for 1200 metres, indicating the track was 'slow'. The *actual* time for the 1200 metres race at Rosehill on the day he quoted was 1.12.4, so how good was that.

It makes you wonder how the Melbourne clubs could ignore information like that, or, like me, didn't they know what was going on in Sydney?

Anyway, after receiving John Jeff's letter I felt quite deflated because I thought my story on the penetrometer was an 'exclusive'. Nevertheless it did result in the penetrometer coming to Victoria where it was widely adopted and applauded.

THIS GADGET WILL BE A BOON

BRIAN Green, track manager at Sandown, has been using an imported French penetrometer to test the state of the going and he is delighted with the results.

Brian has used the penetrometer for the [illegible] three Sandown [illegible]tings and has found it a big help when making his decision to announce the classification of the track.

"Now I am really looking forward to the winter to use the penetrometer on wet tracks.

"I am sure by the end of the season I will be able to give a more accurate assessment of the track than I have in the past," Brian said.

Tests

The penetrometer was sent to Brian late last year by M. Jean Romanet, of the French Jockey Club, after he had written to him seeking details.

Brian was prompted by my stories in *Truth* after I had seen the penetrometer in action at Longchamp last June.

The penetrometer is a steel implement a little over a metre high which has weight at the top weighing one kilo.

By pulling a trigger the weight drops a full metre causing a steel rod to penetrate the track.

How far the rod goes in depends on the softness or hardness of the track.

The depth of penetration is measured on a graduated scale at the top of the penetrometer.

Then, by keeping records of tests over a period, and comparing them to the times run on each day, a track curator can tell on a particular meeting just how fast the horses will run.

The penetrometer is the best news racing fans have had for years because, at last, it provides a scientific method of giving accurate track readings.

Every race club in this country should have one.

★ Brian Green

★ The penetrometer

★ Maintenon...Hobart Cup favorite.

18

A Dream Comes True

The other *great* day was the day I called the races at Acton Racecourse in Canberra in 1950 when I was 22. I've told you earlier how I called races at Cooma and Adaminaby, but they were small-time affairs compared to Canberra. Races at Acton were conducted by the ACT Jockey Club, the letters ACT standing for Australian Capital Territory, Canberra's official title.

The club had its own permanent racecaller, but the particular meeting I'm talking about was hired out to a sporting organisation which had a licence to run just one meeting a year, the St. Patrick's Racing Club, but the ACT Jockey Club provided the officials such as the stewards, the judge, timekeeper etc.

The job of commentator however was at the discretion of the club that was benefitting from the meeting, and it just happened I was best mates with a fellow called Phil Donnelly, whose father, Clem Donnelly, was President of the St. Pat's Racing Club. Phil had accompanied me on one occasion when I was calling at Braidwood, a small town in southern New South Wales, and he knew I was capable with the microphone and binoculars.

When we got home he said: 'How would you like to call the St. Pat's meeting?'

'That would be great, but how?' I replied.

'I'll tell my dad and you can show him your credentials,' he said.

So it was arranged I meet Mr. Donnelly and the Secretary of the ACT Jockey Club, George O'Neill, and put my case to them.

One of the truest saying in life is: 'It's not *what* you know but *who* you know'. I got the job.

But it was no piece of cake. Canberra racecourse was very primitive. There was no grandstand. The patrons stood on the side of a hill that overlooked the home straight. And that's where I stood. No broadcaster's box for me. Just a microphone fixed on a pole, head-high, and me standing on the side of the hill and struggling to keep upright on the slope. There was no attachment to keep my binoculars steady as all the callers have as part of their equipment today, so you needed a firm hand.

The day was so memorable for me because I was fulfilling a dream. Sure, it wasn't Flemington or Randwick, but Canberra was the capital city of Australia and my home town. Standing there in front of the microphone in my Clark Kent suit (a sporty light blue check with fawn overtones that Superman would have been proud of), I felt I was the epitome of what I expected a metropolitan broadcaster to be—sharp, check patterned suit, voice with a nasal twang. The only thing missing was the snap brim felt hat to complete the picture, but I wasn't into hats. I figured they were for the older guys.

I was happy to get through the day without a mistake but my career as a racecaller was short-lived. In fact that meeting at Canberra was the last time I ever called a race. But that didn't matter, I had achieved a lifelong ambition. Not long afterwards my application to join *The Argus* newspaper was successful and I was off to Melbourne again. But this time I went as a grown man.

I was now 23 years old and capable of looking after myself.

No need to stay with relatives this time. So after short stints at the Post Office Hotel and a boarding house at Preston I settled permanently at Waverley Street in Essendon.

19

Starting At *Truth*

I spent almost six years at *The Argus*, leaving just before the end of 1956. Again luck was in my way. Tom Moon, who had taken over from Jack Elliott as Racing Editor, got word that the No.2 racing man at *Truth* newspaper was leaving to return to his hometown in Sydney. He advised me to hightail it up to *Truth* and make myself available. Tom was a good friend and knew that if I got the job it would mean a promotion for me.

Truth office was only 100 metres or so further up La Trobe Street from *The Argus* so I almost ran there and put myself forward to George Parker, the Racing Editor. I knew George from the races. All the racing writers were pretty close and we got along well together, even though we were rivals and always keen to outdo each other to get that exclusive story.

One of my keenest competitors was Rollo Roylance, who was one of the senior writers on *The Sun*, before he became Racing Editor of the *Sporting Globe*. *The Sun* was the biggest selling daily paper in Melbourne and the main opposition to *The Argus*. Rollo and I were often pitted against each other at the country races where each of us would be responsible for providing a story for our newspaper the next day.

Rollo was six or seven years older than me and well known among the racing people at the country meetings, especially the owners and trainers, who would be the most likely source of any story that was going to come out of the meeting. It seemed to me that every time I looked around Rollo was chatting earnestly to one of these men, or some official, or a bookmaker. I would see him vigorously making notes in his racebook and I would be thinking, 'I wonder what he is onto?'

I would spend a restless night in bed after some of those country meetings waiting until I could get a copy of *The Sun* the next morning to see if Rollo had 'scooped' me. Fortunately, as I recall, Rollo didn't have any better coverage of the meeting than I had in *The Argus*. I eventually concluded that it was his nature to always look busy. I remember him always being on the move, always talking to someone. That's why he was such a good reporter, he never stopped trying.

My days of worrying about getting 'scooped' however were about to come to an end. My hurried trip to the *Truth* office ended successfully with George Parker assuring me I would get the job once his deputy had left. I resigned from *The Argus* and took up my position as No.2 man at *Truth* a few weeks later.

This was a different ball game altogether. *Truth* was a bi-weekly coming out only on Tuesdays and Thursdays compared to *The Argus*, which was printed every day bar Sunday. So while I was always on the look-out for an 'exclusive', I wasn't in competition with the dailies any longer.

At *Truth* we were all about the 'form'. We provided more details about the performances of each horse than any other paper in Melbourne, or in Australia for that matter. The only one comparable was the Sydney based *Sportsman*, and that paper was owned in the same interests as *Truth*. We supplied the Melbourne form for it anyway.

Both *Sportsman* and *Truth* were owned by Ezra Norton, a

Sydney newspaper mogul who published the Sydney *Truth* and the Sydney *Daily Mirror*.

Norton had a reputation as a ruthless employer, sacking people right and left. So when he came to Melbourne, which was rare, everyone in the office was on their best behaviour. The one time he came while I was there he just walked into the Editor's room, said what he had to say, and walked out.

We all gave a sigh of relief because everyone knew of his volatile nature due to the stories that had come down from Sydney about him. We had heard that in one of his staff shake-ups he had sacked 20 reporters in one hit.

And then there was the time he had a fist fight at Randwick races with his fierce competitor Frank Packer, who owned the *Daily Telegraph* and the *Sunday Telegraph*. They were both keen racegoers, horse owners, and Packer was actually on the committee of the Australian Jockey Club. Apparently Norton didn't like the unflattering photos Packer was publishing of him in his newspapers and threw the first punch.

The story goes that there was quite a stoush and that Packer came off the worse for wear. Norton was later forced to apologise to the AJC Committee. But despite his poor reputation I have read that he had a softer side and was known to have helped out staffers who fell on hard times.

About three years after I joined *Truth*, Norton sold the *Mirror* and *Truth* to Rupert Murdoch. This was a turning point for me because George Parker also decided to call it quits. I don't know how old George was at the time but he would have been at least 65, the normal retiring age, so his decision to leave was no surprise. I was duly appointed Racing Editor and my career really took off from that point.

Rupert appointed a new Editor, Jeff Utting, who had a

distinguished career with the Melbourne *Herald*. Jeff continued *Truth*'s investigative and confronting role but also brought a new freshness to the paper and opened its pages to allow for a broader sporting coverage. There was more space for racing editorial, which had previously been almost non-existent, the coverage consisting primarily of the horses' form.

My best opportunities to write stories came through the paper's breeding supplement which carried advertisements for the March yearling sales. My task was to visit the stud farms, inspect the yearlings advertised, and write some editorial about them.

One of the studs was named Kenwyn Park at Rockbank, not far out of Melbourne. It was owned by Mr. W.J. Drever, well known as Melbourne's 'tripe king', because of his string of butcher shops which specialised in offal, especially tripe.

My visit there was memorable because it almost changed the course of my life!

Mr. Drever had two yearling fillies by the in-form sire Orgoglio among his draft for the annual autumn yearling sales conducted by Wright, Stephenson. Orgoglio, a son of the world-famous stallion Nasrullah, was a sprinting sensation in England and had been imported to Australia by the cricketer H.C. 'Slinger' Nitschke to stand at his stud at Nagambie in Victoria.

When I inspected the two fillies at Kenwyn Park Stud I was most impressed by the brown coloured daughter of Wee Cushla, and wrote her up as a gilt-edged racing proposition in the breeding supplement. She was small, but nuggety, with short canons, a typical sprinter. The other filly, a daughter of Gai Filette, was more athletic looking, taller, leaner, a filly you would think had the scope to run a distance—particularly as her grand dam, Gay Helios, had run third to Rising Fast in the 1954 Melbourne Cup.

I really liked those fillies and wondered what it would be like to race one of them. Would Mr. Drever lease one of them to me? Then I had a better idea. What if he would lease one to *Truth* and we would race it for our readers?

I put the suggestion to the Editor, as Utting was a regular racegoer and genuinely interested in the sport. He liked the idea but said he would have to run it past Rupert Murdoch. To support his argument he said he would suggest that any prizemoney (less expenses) won by the horse under the lease, would be donated to the Royal Children's Hospital, a charity of which Rupert's mother, Dame Elisabeth, was the Patron.

But first I had to get Mr. Drever to lease us the horse. He was a good sport and said he would be happy to agree because he would be getting the filly back when the lease expired. Rupert gave the idea the thumbs up, so all that remained was to choose which filly we would take.

I really did like the stocky brown filly out of Wee Cushla but this was a big decision to make. *Truth* would be up for the training fees and all the other associated costs, and there would be the paper's 400,000 readers all expecting the horse to be a winner.

Was I really competent to make the choice? What did I know about horseflesh? I was a racing writer not a bloodstock expert. Sure, I'd studied horses as they paraded at the races and thought I could tell when a horse looked ready to win. But this was different. These fillies were just yearlings, not long broken in.

I decided to call for help. The obvious choice seemed to be to go to the man who would train the filly. Who should we choose? The leading trainers at the time were Angus Armanasco and Brian Courtney, both outstanding men at their profession, but Angus trained at Caulfield and Brian further out at Mentone. For publicity purposes I thought it would be better to have the filly trained at racing's headquarters, Flemington, which was also closer to the *Truth* office.

One trainer there who was having a lot of success was Tony Lopes, famous as the trainer of the champion filly Chicquita who strung together eight wins in a row as a three-year-old including the One Thousand Guineas, Wakeful Stakes and VRC Oaks. But she is best remembered for her many duels with Comic Court whom she ran second to in the 1950 Melbourne Cup. The pair later mated at stud to produce Comicquita, who also finished second in a Melbourne Cup.

I didn't know Tony personally, but I did know that he had just built a state-of-the-art stables on Flemington racecourse which he had named Chicquita Lodge. It seemed an ideal location to house the *Truth* filly when we finally chose her. So I rang Tony, told him of our plans, and asked if he would help me choose the filly from the two I had seen at Kenwyn Park. And if he liked her, would he train her?

Tony agreed so we drove out to Rockbank and met Bill Drever at the stud, in front of the boxes in which the fillies were housed. A stablehand brought the fillies out and paraded them for our inspection. I said I liked them both but deferred any decision to the two older gentlemen who had far more experience.

Tony said the stocky brown Wee Cushla filly looked a dead-set sprinter, after the style of her sire Orgoglio. The other filly, out of Gai Filette, he said was likely to have more longevity and might get an Oaks distance despite her sire being a sprinter. He pointed out that Orgoglio had sired Mintaway, winner of the VRC Oaks two years earlier. Bill Drever added that this filly came from one of his foundation families and he would be happy to have her back when the lease ran out.

So the consensus was that while the Wee Cushla filly was

likely to win early races there would be more mileage, from a publicity point of view, in the Gai Fillette filly, whose appearance and pedigree suggested she would be the more versatile.

Decision made. The chestnut Gai Fillette filly was off to Tony Lopes' stables and the Wee Cushla would go to the yearling sales.

The Wee Cushla filly went through the sale ring in Melbourne and was knocked down to Orgoglio's owner 'Slinger' Nitschke for 600 guineas. He called her Proud Miss.

Next priority was to give the *Truth* filly a suitable name. It was really a no-brainer. She would be called Paper Girl.

You can probably guess how the story turned out. Proud Miss ran third in Adelaide at her first start then won her next 10 races in a row, a record for a two-year-old in Australia. Her run ended when she was second to Birthday Card in the Golden Slipper Stakes at Rosehill.

Paper Girl never won a race.

Had it been the other way around I could have ended up owning *Truth*, not just working for it. Well not really, but it would have enhanced my reputation with Rupert Murdoch and, I'm sure, led to better opportunities.

But that's life and I have never for one moment regretted my life at *Truth*. In fact I loved every minute of it. The horses, the people, the travelling around the word with *Truth*'s Racing Tours… what more could a racing journalist ask for?

There was one thing I missed though. That was the opportunity to write stories. *Truth*'s racing section was primarily a form guide, a list of a horses' past performances. At *The Argus* I had been reporting on daily news, live events, and doing interviews with trainers and jockeys. Every day was exciting.

But at *Truth*, reading through proofs of the form of hundreds of horses and checking them for mistakes could become boring. The bright side to that however was that I became very familiar with the form of the runners in Saturday's races. That put me in a good position when it came to trying to tip the readers a winner.

I had a bit of luck in that regard, winning two or three awards, but not as much as my deputy, John Greensill, who was an expert at finding winners. John was an avid reader of the form proofs and while I might have found that boring at times, John thrived on it. John won several awards for his tipping and had many followers.

So to ease that monotony of the form proofs I tried to put more interest into the daily routine at the office. I suggested to the then editor—I forget which one, we had so many—that we produce a racing magazine to tell the stories of the jockeys and trainers and other racing personalities as well as profiling the best horses of the time.

Well, this particular Editor wasn't all that interested in that side of the paper so he passed me off to the Managing Director of the company that published *Truth*, Southdown Press. His name was Brian Morris and he *was* a racing man. Brian liked the idea and after he had tossed it around with the other directors it was agreed to produce it provided it could be done without hiring extra staff and no added cost to the company.

I guaranteed that the advertising revenue would cover the costs involved so we were off and running, except that we didn't have a name for the magazine. My first choice was to call it 'Winning Post', which was acceptable to everyone except the artist who had to design the cover.

He said the words wouldn't fit across the page in the size he wanted. My next choice was 'Bred To Win' which I thought would appeal to breeders as well as punters and, after all, the breeders were going to be the main source of the advertising revenue.

Brian Morris agreed, but I know he was a bit disappointed because he believed the magazine would sell better if the name was directed more to helping punters back winners. He was right, but the artist stuck solid that Winning Post was too long.

So *Bred To Win* it was and it was successful. It was the first magazine to produce photos of racehorses in full colour, due to the advanced technology of Southdown Press' printing processes. Our competitors, *Racetrack* and *Turf Monthly*, were still printing their photos in black and white.

The first edition of *Bred To Win*, with a beautiful colour action photo of Rain Lover on the cover was a great success and the Directors of Southdown Press gave it the go-ahead to be produced each quarter, spring, summer, autumn and winter.

As it progressed, we expanded the coverage to include articles written by other members of Rupert Murdoch's stable of newspapers, including Pat Farrell of the Sydney *Daily Telegraph* and Joe Lyons of the *Daily Mirror*. Ross du Bourg, Australia's most knowledgeable writer on racehorse pedigrees, was brought in to join me as joint Editor.

So we had a very prestigious racing magazine and it was well received. It was published for four years until Southdown Press pulled the plug on it due to competition from the company's two best sellers, *New Idea* and *TV Week*. Both these weekly magazines were flying with *New Idea* selling more than one million copies a week and *TV Week* doing close to 900,000.

In the rush to get these two magazines on the streets every inch of Southdown Press' printing facilities was required to work non-stop. There just wasn't room any more for a specialist magazine like *Bred To Win*, whose circulation was only a small fraction of the 'big two'.

I was sorry to see it go as it was a classy production which presented racing as an important part of the Australian economy, not just a gambling medium. But by this time *Truth* had increased the space allotted to racing editorial, so I was still able to indulge my passion for writing about the sport.

20

The Page 3 Girls

Truth continued to prosper as an investigative newspaper and the racing coverage received another boost when Rupert Murdoch appointed Roger 'Solly' Chandler as Editor in 1964. Rupert was looking for a hotshot London journalist-executive to run his new baby *The Australian*, which was to be Australia's first national newspaper, and he had induced Solly to come to Australia to do the job.

But the feeling among Rupert's advisors was that the first Editor of a national newspaper should be Australian-born. Rupert gave way and appointed Maxwell Newton, an experienced economic journalist who had worked for the Department of Treasury in Canberra. Solly Chandler was not forgotten however, and Rupert sent him to Melbourne to take over *Truth*.

Truth was languishing with a circulation of around 200,000. In a little over a year Solly had lifted that figure to more than 400,000 with his sensational headlines and revealing stories about corrupt police and politicians, and any other public figures who fell foul of his vitriolic pen.

Solly also introduced two other outstanding features which helped to considerably boost *Truth*'s circulation—The Page 3 Girl and Heart Balm. The Page 3 girl was immensely popular. It was the photo of a glamourous bare-breasted model whose charms were not inconsequential, in fact, they were always more than ample, and therein lay their appeal. Another factor was that *Truth* was the only newspaper that dared to publish such revealing details of the feminine anatomy.

But not everyone was impressed, particularly the Under Secretary in the Victorian Government, Sir Arthur Rylah, who declared such pictures indecent, and ruled they could only be shown if a black strip was painted across the girls' nipples. These black bands became known as 'Rylah bars' and remained in force until Solly Chandler convinced Sir Arthur that he was living in the Dark Ages.

This change of heart may not have been so difficult to achieve as you might think.

Solly was famous for the long lunches he shared with politicians and heads of industry. In fact, he invited me to one of them, at Ress' Hotel in Collins Street. The owner, Mick Ress, was a popular figure on the Melbourne social circuit and the downstairs dining room, which featured red leather furnishings amid softly lit surrounds, was one of the city's finest culinary locations.

I remember the occasion quite well, mainly for the duration of the meal, which lasted for the whole of the afternoon, and for the amount of red wine that was consumed, so much in fact that I still wonder how I got through the next day with such a hangover. The only other person I can recall at that lunch was Sir Arthur Rylah himself. He and Solly didn't always agree but they respected each other and had long conversations on the politics of the day.

Eventually *Truth* was able to publish the photos of the Page 3 girls without the Rylah bars and they became synonymous with the paper. One of the most popular exhibits was a Hawaiian girl Solly christened Alexandra The Great because of her 48-inch bust. She became so popular with *Truth* readers that Solly had her flown out from Honolulu to do a promotional tour for the paper.

That's the kind of operator Solly was. He knew what the public wanted and the paper boomed because of his insight. *Truth* reached its peak circulation of 404,000 under Solly's Editorship and one of the stories that helped to get it there was headlined 'Drunken Duncan'.

The Duncan referred to was Duncan Stevens, the captain of the destroyer HMAS *Voyager* which collided with the aircraft carrier HMAS *Melbourne* during exercises off Jervis Bay in New South Wales. As a consequence the *Voyager* was sunk and 82 sailors drowned.

A Royal Commission was held into the incident and as a result the captain of the *Melbourne*, John Robertson, was criticised for not warning the *Voyager* of the danger it was in. Robertson was banned from ever taking a ship to sea again.

Fast forward two years: Solly's Secretary, Pearl Allen, walks into his office and tells him she's got news on the *Voyager* disaster. Pearl told Solly a friend she had worked with in a previous employment had a son-in-law who was highly ranked in the Navy and worked alongside Duncan Stevens, captain of the *Voyager*. The friend told her that Stevens was close to being an alcoholic and that at a cocktail party reception in Hong Kong had to be carried out.

Pearl's source later repeated the story to Solly who splashed it on Page 1 of *Truth* under the heading Drunken Duncan. The story sparked a sensation in Canberra political circles and led to the formation of a second Royal Commission into the collision between the two ships.

Solly was subpoenaed to appear at the hearing where he was told he was required to name the source of his information. Failure to do so would incur a heavy fine, or a jail term, or both.

Solly refused, and instead embarked on a 10-minute defence of the freedom of the Press and its right to protect its sources. His eloquence allowed him to escape with a $2000 fine.

This second Royal Commission found that Captain Stevens was unfit to command the *Voyager* due to ill health and absolved Captain Robertson from the blame.

I relay that story to show that *Truth* wasn't just a 'dirty rag' as some of its detractors would have it, but a responsible paper breaking stories that were in the public interest. Sure it was a bit on the sleazy side with its accent on sex and crime but sex sold newspapers. The saving grace for *Truth*, in the eyes of the public, was its Racing Guide.

If you asked anybody why they bought *Truth* the answer would always be 'for the racing guide'. Of course that wasn't really true, but it covered up their embarrassment for buying a paper that many considered 'naughty'. If you bought it for the racing guide however, you were above criticism. It was universally acknowledged that *Truth* had the best form guide in Melbourne.

In the 37 years I spent there I think we had about 20 Editors. Some were good, some very good, and two or three not very good at all. But the ones that couldn't cut it didn't last long. The best of all, no doubt, was Chandler. Doubling the circulation with his daring and innovative ideas like Heart Balm and the Page 3 Girl was only half the story.

One of his biggest triumphs was the introduction of 'The Big Swim', a race across Port Phillip Heads from Portarlington to Frankston, a distance of around 22 nautical miles, or 40km.

The idea was hatched in a pub (of course) where Solly was indulging in his favourite tipple, a Hine Brandy with his ace reporter Jack Ayling and a couple of other journos. According to Jack, as he wrote in his book *Nothing But The Truth*, Solly asked him if anyone had ever swum across Port Phillip Bay, and was told it had never been attempted. To which Solly replied 'Let's do it'.

Jack was put in charge of organising the event which became a full-time job for him in the days leading up. One of the big issues was having metal cages constructed for the entrants to swim in, Port Phillip Bay reputedly having its share of man-eating sharks.

The event attracted five starters but none was able to finish. From that point of view the race was disappointing, but the event had caught the public's attention and plans were quickly made to repeat the race the following year.

This time Jack had been able to secure the entry of the world's best female endurance swimmer, Linda McGill. She had just swum the English Channel in the fastest time ever for a woman. A field of nine lined up and Linda beat them all home in a time of 12 hours 54 minutes. Three other swimmers finally made it to the shore but had to be taken to Frankston Hospital before recovering from the ordeal.

According to Jack's story a crowd of 50,000 people were waiting on Frankston Pier to greet the swimmers who were able to make it. That's the kind of story that made *Truth* one of Melbourne's most read newspapers and why Solly Chandler was one of its more significant Editors.

21

Gateway To The World

Luckily for me Solly was a racing man. He had been a regular racegoer in England and he liked a bet so he knew all about form guides. One of the first things he did as the new Editor was to call me into his office to have a chat about the way we presented the form. He asked: 'Why do you only have three last-start figures before the horse's name?'

'Because that's the way it's always been done,' I replied.

'Well we are going to change that,' he said. 'We are going to have six numbers. And we are going to include the trainer's name in the race fields.'

'But there isn't enough room,' I replied.

'Don't worry about that,' he said, 'we'll simply expand the width of the columns.'

So it was done. Within weeks every other paper had altered its style to copy ours.

I owe a lot to Solly. Through him I got to report on all the major racing carnivals throughout Australia and, eventually, the world. He simply said to me not long after he took over: 'Let me know when you are leaving for Sydney, Ron.'

'I beg your pardon?' I answered.

'For Sydney, for the Easter carnival,' he added.

'But I don't go to Sydney,' I said. 'We don't cover the Sydney races.'

‘Well, we do now,’ was his reply. ‘We are a national paper and I want you to go to all the major carnivals round Australia.’

It was a great opportunity and helped expand my racing knowledge a great deal. The things I learned in Sydney, Brisbane, Adelaide, and later in Perth, I was able to pass on to our readers. It was in Sydney I got to know Tommy Smith and he became a wonderful source of information.

I first met him at the spring Carnival at Randwick in 1965. Up until then I had just been one of the Press pack listening to him giving his after-race report on his various trips to Melbourne. I had never been introduced to him and consequently had never spoken to him.

But one day at Randwick I happened to be standing next to him as we ordered a drink from the bar. He turned to me and said: ‘I’ll win the Derby today, Ron.’ I was surprised because I didn’t think he knew me. I remember it clearly though, because then he added: ‘Prince Grant will win the Derby.’

I couldn’t believe my luck, getting a tip from Tommy. I went into the betting ring and there was Prince Grant at 50/1. There were only eight runners and Tommy had half the field—Conclave and Pyramus, both at 9/1, Barham Star at 33/1 and Prince Grant at 50s. The favourite was Fair Summer, long odds on at 2/7.

I don’t exactly remember what I had on Prince Grant, probably One Pound each-way which was equivalent to $2 each-way in today’s currency… enough to put on a longshot.

Prince Grant bolted in. He won by eight lengths with the hot favourite Summer Fair finishing fifth after virtually pulling himself into the ground. I don’t know how Tommy did it, but he knew he had the best stayer in the race.

Prince Grant went on to have a stellar autumn campaign.

He won five of his seven starts including the Sydney Cup, Chipping Norton Stakes and Queen Elizabeth Stakes, and earned the title of the best weight-for-age horse in Australia at the time.

As the years went on I got to know Tommy quite well and he was the source of many stories that appeared in *Truth*. He knew the value of publicity and would always pick up the phone if you rang. Unlike one leading Melbourne trainer who was always 'in the shower' or 'having breakfast' or 'having dinner'.

A funny thing happened on one of those trips to Sydney. It was not long after Rupert Murdoch sold *Truth* to Mark Day and Owen Thompson, two of his former executives who got together the $1million they needed to buy the paper.

It was tough going in those early days working out of rented premises in West Melbourne, but Mark and Owen did keep up the practice of sending me to cover all the major racing carnivals. So, comes Golden Slipper Day and I've got the OK to go to Rosehill.

Because money was tight it was agreed I would go up and back in the one day. I could cope with that. So I get an early flight to Sydney and plan to stop off for a coffee break at the closest hotel to Circular Quay Railway Station. From there I would take the train to Rosehill.

I can't recall the name of the hotel, I think it has changed in the meantime, but then it was the most expensive 5-star hotel in Sydney. But just for a cup of coffee why not have the best?

So I'm waiting for a cab at Sydney airport when I find I'm standing next to Ernie Sigley, who had an afternoon radio show on 3AW. I'd never met Ernie but I knew of him (who in Melbourne didn't?). Ernie loved his racing and he knew me because I was also doing some work at 3AW. Ernie says to me: 'Where are you going, Ron.' I tell him Circular Quay, so he says 'I've got a limo coming to pick me up, so I can drop you off.'

That suited me, so the next minute this giant limo arrives and the uniformed driver ushers us in. We drive to Circular Quay, right up to the main entrance of the hotel which opened onto a huge reception area. I could see people sitting there with tea or coffee and watching the arrivals through the giant plate glass windows.

I get out of the limo carrying my luggage, a portable typewriter and a pair of binoculars, and head into the reception area. The next thing this tall bloke jumps up from a chair and shouts: 'What the f*****g hell are you doing here?' It's Owen Thompson!

He must have got the shock of his life when he sees me arriving in such style and why wasn't I at the races anyway? I must admit I was surprised to see Owen myself. I had no idea he was going to be in Sydney that weekend.

I quickly explained I was just stopping off for a coffee and my friend Ernie had been kind enough to give me a lift. Fortunately this placated Owen who, I'm sure, had visions of me presenting an expense account for a limousine from Mascot to Rosehill and for an overnight stay in a 5-star hotel.

Owen was very strict when checking expenses. I remember one day he asked a reporter if he could borrow his Melbourne *Herald*. When the reporter replied he didn't have a copy Owen exploded: 'Well, you should have, you bloody well charge for one on your expenses. Don't f*****g do it again.'

Under Mark Day and Owen's leadership *Truth* prospered for several years due to its wide coverage of news including hard-hitting stories on crime and politics, as well as tell-all stories on personalities in the entertainment industry. It also benefited from the revenue it received from massage parlour advertisements.

These advertisements were received on a cash basis and had

to be paid for before the paper would print them. Of course the word 'massage' was really a euphemism for 'brothel' or 'prostitute' and it was a source of great enjoyment for us staffers to watch these attractive girls arrive in their ridiculously high heels come in to lodge their copy.

So while *Truth* may have had its sleazy side it was also a very serious newspaper. It investigated some the biggest issues of the day, sometimes exposing new evidence, and getting itself involved in criminal affairs. *Truth* was known as 'the people's paper' and aggrieved persons would often come to it with their problems.

One of the biggest stories with which *Truth* was involved, was the escape from Pentridge by Ronald Ryan and Peter Walker in 1965. Ryan had shot dead a warder, George Hodson, during the escape and the hunt for him and Walker was national news. *Truth* got a 'scoop' when Ryan, while on the move, wrote to the Editor a long and vitriolic letter condemning the Victorian Police Department and the judiciary.

The story was on the front page of *Truth* and other sensational stories followed, boosting the circulation of the paper considerably. The escapees were finally caught in January 1966, 17 days after their escape. Ryan was convicted of murder and hung at Pentridge Prison on 3 February 1967. Walker got 12 years for manslaughter.

I tell this story of Ryan and Walker firstly because I became involved in it and secondly because I later made a friend of one of the barristers appearing at the trial of the two men.

How did I get involved? Well, eight days after the shooting of the Pentridge warder, police rounded up and arrested seven people for harbouring Ryan and Walker who were still on the run. Six of the seven were released on bail but one, a young mother, couldn't make the bail money.

My colleague at *Truth*, and best mate, Jack Ayling, who was reporting the story, got the tipoff that she was distressed over being apart from her baby daughter.

Jack passed this news on to Solly Chandler, who had a ready solution for the woman's difficulty. *Truth* would bail her out. He told Jack he would get him the 2000 pounds bail money and Jack could do the paperwork required. Only there was one big catch. This was Tuesday 27 December and the banks were closed for the holiday. Where was the money going to come from?

But this didn't faze Solly. 'The races are on at Moonee Valley today, aren't they Jack?'

'Yes,' replied Jack.

'Well, Ron Taylor will be there, give him a ring and ask him to see if one of the bookmakers will lend him the money until tomorrow when the banks are open.'

So I am at Moonee Valley when the *Truth* phone in the Press Room rings. Jack tells me what Solly wants, which I didn't think would be a problem because I knew all the rails bookmakers, some better than others, and had no hesitation approaching them.

The leader of the ring was Albert Smith. I got on well with Albert, he was a gentleman, as were the others, though a couple might have been a little rough around the edges. I told Albert the story and his reaction was just what I expected. He simply turned to his clerk who was taking the money for the tickets Albert was writing and said: 'Take 2000 out of the bag and give it to Ron will you, John.'

It was as simple as that. Albert knew *Truth* would be good for the money and that it would be there at settling the following day. It was.

Solly Chandler arranged for the cash to be withdrawn from the bank and I took it to the Victorian Club in Queen Street where the bookies did their settling and handed it over.

In the meantime, back at Moonee Valley, I rang Jack Ayling and arranged to meet him at the Sabloniere Hotel (*Truth*'s watering hole) to hand over the money. Solly was also there when I arrived and he quickly arranged for photographer John Murie to accompany Jack on his mission of mercy.

Next stop for Jack was the Fairleigh Police Station to lodge the money and pick up the release papers for the bailout. Then to Fairleigh Women's Prison to present the papers and pick up the young woman.

According to Jack she was a bit bewildered by what was happening but very relieved when he was able to drop her off at her home and reunite her with her baby. As you would imagine the story, with pictures, was all over the front page of the next edition of *Truth*. Again, this shows that *Truth* had a heart, and wasn't the 'gutter rag' that some people had ignorantly tabbed it.

22

The Regal Vista Ring-In

The biggest story I ever wrote at *Truth* concerned the ringing-in (substituting) of the crack racehorse Regal Vista for the poorly performed Royal School at Casterton in 1972. The story was on the front page of *Truth* and billed as 'A *Truth* Exclusive on the Racing Sensation of the Century'.

And sensational it certainly was. The gist of it was that I had discovered the whereabouts of Regal Vista who had mysteriously disappeared after being sold a few weeks before the Munthan Handicap at Casterton.

On that day, 12 May, a horse racing under the name of Royal School won the Muntham Handicap by three lengths, backed from 25/1 to 7/4.

Subsequent events were to prove that horse was actually Regal Vista, a brilliant sprinter who held the record for five furlongs at Moonee Valley, and only the year before had finished third to two champion sprinters Dual Choice and Tango Miss in the Oakleigh Plate.

Royal School, on the other hand, was a duffer. At his four previous starts he had finished last, second last, last and second last, all in low grade country races. The plot to stage the ring-in was hatched by a fellow called Rick Renzella who managed a used-car yard in Brighton.

Renzella owned a few horses which he raced with moderate success, but he wasn't in the racing limelight. I had never met him. One day, out of the blue, I get a phone call from him inviting me to visit his stud farm at Toolern Vale to inspect a new stallion he had just purchased from a stud in New South Wales.

He told me he was inviting all the racing Pressmen because he wanted to get the maximum publicity for his new stallion leading up to the stud season. The inspection was to be held on a Sunday and he said it would be a relaxing afternoon with entertainment and plenty of food and drink.

Sunday was my day off, but I thought, why not? I could take my wife Lola and a day out in the country would be a nice break.

Not long after we arrived however it became apparent that I was the only Pressman to turn up. So Renzella gave me a personal tour of the property while showing off his new stallion, King Tudor. By the end of the afternoon we had become quite pally and promised to keep in touch.

I never encountered him again until a few months later when rumours started flying that there had been a ring-in at Casterton.

This time it was me chasing him, not the other way around. Renzella had become the centre of attention being the registered owner of Royal School who had staged this remarkable turnaround in form to win the Muntham Handicap.

I had his phone number, and he agreed to give me an interview. But only on condition that he could read the copy before it was printed.

This wasn't my usual mode of operation but because it was such a big story I agreed. Then the cloak and dagger stuff started. After the story was written I had to meet him in Market Street, an out-of-the-way street that ran from Collins Street down to Flinders Street.

I found Rick sitting in his car alongside his solicitor, Brian Cash. This was serious stuff. Not only did Renzella have to approve the story it had to be ticked off by Mr. Cash. No big deal there because the story was straightforward and dealt mainly with Renzella's betting activities in the past.

By now news had leaked out that Renzella had won $33,570 on the Daily Double at Casterton by linking the Field in the first leg with Royal School in the second leg. The double paid $111.90 for a 50-cent ticket, odds of almost 220/1.

By any standards this was a huge win on a small country race. Questions were being asked.

But this didn't faze Renzella. In the car he told me: 'I don't know what all the fuss is about. I have made some big plunges in the past and there has been no inquiry.' This time however, there *was* an inquiry. A big one.

As the inquiry progressed it became evident that Renzella had been involved in the sale of Regal Vista only a week before the running of the Muntham Handicap. It transpired he had been eyeing off Regal Vista for some weeks as a potential ring-in horse because of his likeness to Royal School, a horse he had bought a few months before for $350.

But he didn't want his name involved in the purchase of Regal Vista so he conned two associates into buying the horse. It was merely a ploy. These two guys never ever saw Regal Vista. The sale was completed through an agent.

After Royal School had won so easily at Casterton a connection began to be drawn with Regal Vista who had been surprisingly scratched from a race at Moonee Valley six days before the Munthan Handicap.

When questioned, the new owners said they had sent the horse to Perth where he would continue his career. The stewards could find no trace of this movement and the mystery began to deepen.

Because I had developed a friendly association with Renzella that day at Toolern Vale he kept me in the picture with what was going on. If the stewards had summoned him to an inquiry he would ring and let me know. I recall on one day the stewards had chosen to interview him at a country racecourse on a Sunday. He said it might be interesting for me to be there.

Because it was my day off I suggested to my wife she might like to come and she said that it might be nice if we also took her mother along for the ride. That was OK by me so off we went to Pakenham Racecourse and pulled up somewhere close to the winning post. I was immediately approached by a smartly dressed young man in a snap brim hat who stepped up to the driver's side window.

'What are you doing here?' was the greeting. Before I could answer a voice calls out from the back seat: 'It's got nothing to do with me, I've just come for the ride.' It's my mother-in-law all flustered and wondering what's going on.

I tell the young man, who I recognise is Mr. Bill Brewer the steward in charge of the inquiry, that I have come to hear his report after he has questioned Rick Renzella. He tells me I am not supposed to be there, and I wonder if he thinks I am in league with Renzella.

This could have been understandable because, thanks to Renzella's tip-offs, I did keep bobbing up wherever the stewards were involved looking for evidence, like stable inspections and checking out Royal School's brands.

Perhaps having two women in my car satisfied Mr. Brewer as to my intentions, because he just directed me to park somewhere out of the way. He said he would let me know if there was anything to report after he had spoken to Renzella.

Whatever they said however was not for the Press. But I still got my story, reporting on the secret location for the interview and the fact that Renzella was still very much the focus of their intentions.

The steward's investigation went on day after day until eventually on 4 July, almost two months after the race, they finalised their case. Renzella was disqualified for life. His trainer, Ross Afflick, received the same penalty while the jockey, Stephen Wood, got two years.

Regal Vista was still missing. His owners said he was spelling in Western Australia but no one could find any record of the horse having left Victoria. It was generally assumed he was dead, with the most popular theory being that he had been fed to the crayfish in Portland.

The mystery was solved when I got an unexpected phone call from Renzella telling me he had Regal Vista and that the horse would prove his innocence in the case. He said he had bought the horse from his mate Jim Doumtes and wanted to produce it in public alongside Royal School.

He said that by showing off the two horses side by side the stewards, and anyone else who cared, would see that it was Royal School that had won the Munthan Handicap, not Regal Vista as most people believed.

So he invites me to come to a property at Cranbourne, with a photographer, to take pictures of the two horses together. I must say I was one of those who believed Regal Vista would never be found, so this revelation from Renzella was sensational.

The question I then had to ask myself was: how would I know that the horse he produced was really Regal Vista, and not some look-alike to bolster his case? But I had two things in my favour that I knew would help me make a positive identification.

Firstly, Regal Vista had a prominent scar on his rump. It was in the shape of a Y, a legacy of being pierced by a steel rod in a float accident when he was young. Secondly, I recalled being at a racing conference in Tokyo where an official from America presented a paper on the identification of racehorses in the United States.

He pointed out that the racing authority there had appointed the Pinkerton Detective Agency to photograph the night eyes on the inside of a horse's forelegs and attach this to its registration papers to confirm its identity. He made the point that the night eyes, or chestnuts as we call them, are like the fingerprints of humans. He said that no two sets of night eyes were alike.

So I went to our files at *Truth* and dug out every photograph of Regal Vista that I could find to look for those chestnuts. Fortunately one of the pictures had a very clear shot of his offside foreleg showing the chestnut clearly. It was the shape of an upside-down comma, round at the bottom with the tail at the top. It was very distinct and I had no trouble making an exact copy of it.

I was ready to go, but I felt uneasy about this new development. Renzella was in a corner and could be using me and *Truth* in some ploy that would divert suspicion from himself. So I rang Brian McGuire, a respected bloodstock agent who had been involved in the sale of Regal Vista, and a man who knew the horse well, and asked him to come with me.

I also got hold of Jack Ayling, *Truth*'s crime reporter, and asked him to come as a witness. I didn't think Renzella would dud me, as he had been straight in our conversations all along, but I was taking no chances.

The meeting was arranged for 4pm on Wednesday 21 June so we picked up *Truth* photographer John Keesing and headed to Cranbourne. Renzella met us at the gate into the property with the news that Regal Vista had not yet arrived. 'He is coming by float from Western Australia and should be here soon,' he said.

He then directed us to wait down the end of a lane about 200 yards away and said he would come and get us when the horse arrived. I didn't like the sound of this but went along with it anyway.

So we drove to the end of the lane and parked where we were still able to have a view of the gate into the property. We sat and sat some more. It started to get dark and my fears that something was wrong heightened.

Finally, after about three hours, a light went on at the property and a few minutes later Renzella came up and said the float had arrived and would we follow him. We entered the property and parked outside a barn, or small stable and waited for the next move. Renzella came up and said he would bring Regal Vista out for our inspection.

He led out a tall horse wearing a green canvas rug and paraded it up and down. It didn't look like Regal Vista to me and Brian McGuire just shook his head. Renzella grinned and said 'Royal School' and took the horse back into the barn.

He came back with another horse wearing a similar green rug. This time he took the rug off. We were shocked. The horse was in a pitiful condition. I wrote afterwards in *Truth*: 'His ribs were showing through and his coat was rough and unbrushed. He flinched and pulled away at attempts to pat him.'

The horse was certainly in a bad way. In fact, he looked a bag of bones. But he was calm and allowed Brian McGuire to examine his teeth and run his hands down his forelegs. Brian was convinced. 'This is Regal Vista,' he said.

But I still had my doubts. I had looked for the scar on his rump and, while it was there, it looked to me as if it had been recently cut into the horse's flesh. It was puffy, and open, and raw looking.

I put this observation to Renzella and he replied it was because the horse had been rubbing against the back of the float on his long trip across the Nullabor.

To allay any further doubts I looked at the horse's forelegs to see those distinctive chestnuts. There it was—the final proof. On the inside of the off foreleg was this tear-shaped chestnut. It was identical with the one I had seen in the photograph of Regal Vista.

So, mystery solved we returned to *Truth* where I wrote my story and Keesing printed his pictures. The next issue of *Truth* blazoned the headline 'We find Regal Vista'. Then it was up to Renzella to pursue his case with the stewards.

He produced both Regal Vista and Royal School to them, but instead of helping his case as he hoped it proved to be his undoing. The stewards then had no doubt it was Regal Vista who had won the race at Casterton and proceeded to deal out racing justice.

Then the police stepped in and charged Renzella and some of the others with conspiring to cheat and defraud.

I was called as a witness at their trial to give evidence about finding Regal Vista at Cranbourne. The upshot was that Renzella was sentenced to two years imprisonment. The others were either acquitted or released on good behaviour bonds.

Renzella served only three months as I recall. He had a rare skin disease that required a special treatment not available in prison. After his release he promised to give me the full story behind the ring-in. I met him for one last time in one of Melbourne's outer suburbs but when I produced my notebook he changed his mind. He said he would tell the story one day, but he would write it himself. He never did.

He died in June 2019, and, as far as I know, the full story has died with him. But I must say, that for the short time that I knew him, I didn't find him a bad character. Yes, he was a crook, but cheating the bookies with a ring-in was a game with him—using his wits against theirs. What he didn't consider was how much his actions hurt other people.

He did cause me some sleepless nights wondering what was coming next, but he was always helpful in giving me interviews and keeping me abreast of his dealings with the stewards. For a reporter like me he was good copy, but I know that doesn't excuse his behaviour outside the law. Ricky paid the penalty for that by doing time in prison and being warned off all racecourses for life.

I have mentioned that I became a friend of one of the barristers involved in the trial of Ronald Ryan and Peter Walker over the murder of Pentridge warder George Hodson. I didn't know him at the time, but seven years later I met Philip Opas QC at the trial of Rick Renzella.

I had been subpoenaed to give evidence on behalf of the Crown and Opas was there defending Renzella. He put me through a long interrogation about the story I had written in *Truth* about Renzella producing the horse to me after everyone thought it was dead. I could only tell him the *Truth* of what happened that evening, irrespective of whether it helped Renzella's case or not.

The trial ended with Renzella being found guilty of conspiracy to cheat and defraud, and I never expected to have anything further to do with Mr. Opas. But a few years later he came up to me at the races and told me he had written a book about the ring-in and asked me if I would write the Foreword to it.

I said I would be quite happy to, so, over the next couple of weeks we had a few meetings and got to know each other better. One day he said to me: 'Did you ever play football?'

‘Yes, I used to love it,’ I said.

‘Well,’ he said, ‘how would you like to come and have a kick with me?’

I was a bit surprised at this turn the conversation had taken. I was now 62 or 63 and hadn’t kicked a footy for years. And Philip was about 10 years older than me.

Philip went on to explain that at lunchtime each Friday he and a barrister friend would go down to the MCG, slip into the changerooms and get into their footy gear, jumper, shorts, socks, boots… the whole outfit. Then they would walk across to nearby Yarra Park and kick the Sherrin end to end.

‘Unfortunately,’ continued Philip, ‘my friend has moved on and I am left without a partner. Would you come and join me?’

I was flattered to be asked, but I hadn’t kicked a footy since I played in a game with the racing writers against the racing officials (or was it the jockeys?) about 30 years previously. But I had always kept my jumper, red and black, white shorts, red and black socks, and my footy boots.

I don’t know why, maybe I thought I would get another game somewhere, but there they were, my togs, locked away in a cupboard. So I told Philip I would be happy to join, and in fact, was looking forward to it. All went well, we did a few drop kicks and torpedo punts, took a few marks, and generally had a good time.

I think what impressed me most was getting into the hallowed rooms of the MCG. For all I know I might have been sitting on the same bench as Ron Barassi or Norm Smith. And then showering, suiting up and going back to the office.

I don’t know how Philip did it. He never explained it to me, but I assumed because he had been a member of the Old Melburnians Football Club he had that privilege. Anyway I didn’t ask questions, just accepted my good luck.

You might think that was the end of the story of my sporting activities with Philip, but no, there was more to come. At the end of the footy season, and after we had put our togs back in mothballs, Philip asked if I would like to join him at the nets and have a bat and a bowl.

As well as being an accomplished footballer Philip was also more than handy at cricket. At the age of 81 he represented Australia in a Veterans international touring cricket side as a wicket-keeper.

So back we go to the MCG and this time Philip has a barrister friend to accompany him. So there are three of us. There are no creams or whites, just take your jacket off and do your best. I don't know what part of the MCG we occupied but it was probably underneath the grandstand. It was a huge area and you could give the ball a decent whack.

I had never played much cricket as a kid but I knew the rudiments of the game and fancied myself a bit as a fast bowler. The last time I had held a bat in my hand would have been with the racing writers in one of our social matches against the jockeys. But that was back in the early '60s and here we are in 1992 or 1993.

Philip throws me the ball and says, 'Let's see what you can do'. His friend is facing up at the other end of the pitch so I let one go as fast as I can. 'Good,' says Philip, 'keep going.' I've got the taste for it now, so I keep coming in faster and faster.

I don't know how many overs I bowled but it was quite a few, because when I got home I complained to Lola about feeling a bit sore in the groin. 'Don't worry,' she says, 'you can have your tea sitting on the couch.'

Next morning I could not get out of bed. Lola rings the doctor who says get him around here and I'll have a look at him. Somehow I get dressed and Lola bundles me into the car. The doctor takes a look and says: 'You've got a double hernia. You'll have to see a specialist.' So he arranges the appointment and the specialist explains what needs to be done.

'I will need to operate on the groin area on both sides of your abdomen,' says the specialist. 'You will be off work for six weeks.'

Six weeks! That's a life sentence. So there is a lesson there for old blokes like me who think they are Tom Terrific. I never went back to the MCG after that episode but Philip and I kept in contact and remained good friends until his death in 2008.

23

Touring The World

A day at Yarra Glen races in 1973 turned into another life-changing event. It led to me following racing around the world and visiting cities I had previously only read about—London, Paris, New York, Rome, you name it, I didn't miss many.

It all began so casually. I was leaning over a fence watching horses in the mounting yard at Pakenham when I was approached by a young man who introduced himself as Jim Canny, Manager of Greyhound Tours. He said he was organising a tour to the 1974 English Derby and would like me to lead it.

I didn't quite know what he mean by 'lead' it, so he explained that I would go along with the group, together with my wife, and act in a public relations role, just seeing that everyone was happy and getting full enjoyment from their tour.

It sounded pretty cushy to me so I asked: 'What do you get out of it?' He said his company would advertise the tour in *Truth* telling people that I would be the Tour Leader and about the great races and wonderful places they would see.

This sounded pretty good to me as I had been overseas only once before, in 1969 to the Eighth Asian Racing Conference in Tokyo. I was 40 then and quite old to be a first-time traveller. But that's what it was like in those days for kids of my generation. Parents didn't have the money to send their children overseas and it was too costly to try to do it yourself on the wages you were getting.

I put the proposition to *Truth*'s Editor-In-Chief, Ian Rae, who was very supportive. He ticked it off with the paper's senior management and the tour was on. And what a tour it was. Thirty-two people signed up for the 25 days at a cost of $1140. It was unbelievable value, the airfare alone would have been more than that.

It was a huge success, but there were some incidents that caused me headaches and tested my patience. It started just after we booked into our hotel in Rome, the magnificent Leonardo da Vinci. After the long flight everyone was anxious to get some rest including two young guys who were sharing a room.

In the bathroom they found what they thought were two toilets, a conventional one and another that looked like a wash basin. They had never seen a bidet before. So they started experimenting turning on the bidet's taps and, watching the water flow in. Then they left the room to take a nap.

Next thing one of them feels his bed move. It feels like its floating. He looks down and sees the room is flooded with water. Rushing to the bathroom he finds that the stopper at the bottom of the bidet is closed allowing the water to overflow. What next? He starts looking for his Tour Leader.

I hear the sorry story, how he thought the water would automatically turn itself off when the bowl was full. Wrong. So I have to inform the hotel manager. He is not impressed but quickly issues orders for the maids to get buckets and mops to clean up the mess. The maids were not impressed either. I heard one say as she walked past me 'useless Australian bastards'.

That wasn't the only bidet misadventure we had. The next one would have been funny if it hadn't been so embarrassing for the poor bugger involved. After we left Rome we flew to London and stayed at a very nice hotel called The White House. Also staying there was a Melbourne bookmaker who had made the trip privately to see the Derby.

My group was going to Paris that weekend to see the French Oaks and one of our members had decided not to go. So we had a spare seat on the plane as well as accommodation and race tickets that had been paid for. I suggested to the bookie he might like to join us. So he did.

The hotel in Paris wasn't all that flash but the bathrooms were OK with the usual toilet and bidet. Now the bookie had never seen a bidet before, either, but he thought he knew what it was for. Wrong. I got the story when he came to me at breakfast the morning after our arrival looking a bit sheepish. He said: 'Ron, you know them Bardot things, I did No.2 in the No.1 and had to spend the whole night pushing it down the hole with a pencil.'

Fortunately there were no repercussions but I realised the group needed a lecture on European plumbing. I was no expert but was able to warn them to check out every appliance in the bathroom before using it and, if not sure, check with the management.

But there were still mistakes. Before the French Oaks one lady decided she needed a hair set to look her best. After this was attended to she decided she needed a bath before getting into her finery. So she leans over the tub and turns on the tap. Unfortunately this move activated the shower and water cascaded down on her head. Hair set gone.

There were lots of tears, but not all was lost. The other ladies came to her rescue, dried her off and re-set her hair suitably enough for her to get on the bus and enjoy her day at the Oaks. I didn't hear of any more incidents but I'm sure there were some close shaves. No matter how savvy you were there were always challenges in the different bathrooms.

There was never a dull moment on those tours and, somehow, most of them involved Chantilly racecourse which is about 40km from Paris. On our second visit there in 1975 we lost one of our party. He was a lovely bloke who worked for a brewery and was a devout lover of its product. After the last race I checked all the passengers back on the bus for the return to Paris. One was missing.

So we waited half an hour or more for him to turn up, but no appearance. I was really worried because we couldn't leave the racecourse without him. It was a dilemma because all the other passengers were sitting in their seats and getting impatient.

Situation solved when my wife Lola suggested the bus return to Paris while I stayed behind to look for the missing traveller. One of the other passengers volunteered to stay with me, and then the bus took off. Most people had left the course by this time and the bars were closed. We checked the empty grandstands and went through all the toilets. No sign of him.

We asked a couple of gendarmes if they had seen anyone who looked lost—no, they hadn't. It was getting dark and I thought we would have to give up. But if he wasn't on the racecourse, maybe he had gone back to the restaurant, just outside it, where we had stopped for lunch.

So my helper and I left the course and headed for the restaurant. While waiting to cross the busy highway I looked to the left and there 100 metres away I saw this guy in the middle of the road weaving his way between the traffic. It was our man.

My friend and I hurried to meet him and guide him safely to the other side of the road where we took our breath and the questioning began. 'Well, you know that restaurant where we stopped for lunch, they didn't have any beer, they only served wine. I don't drink wine but I did have a couple and it went to my head.

'So when we got to the races I found a big shady tree and lay down and went to sleep. When I woke up everyone had gone. I remembered seeing a big Esso sign on the way into the racecourse so I thought if I go there they will speak English and tell me how to get back to Australia.'

'Well,' I said, 'we have got to get back to Paris first.'

Fortunately we found ourselves almost right outside the Chantilly railway station and there was a train leaving for Paris in a few minutes. Our stop was only a short walk from our hotel and we were quickly inside and sitting at the Bar. Then the doors opened to let in our group which had just arrived.

You can imagine their cries of surprise when they saw we had found our missing friend and had actually beaten them home. Their bus had been held up in the traffic jam of racegoers getting home from Chantilly while our train had accomplished the journey in less than 30 minutes.

On another occasion one of our party was picked up by the gendarmes and locked up on the racecourse. He wasn't impressed, and he had a right to be because he had done nothing wrong. And it was my fault.

I had this habit when we were away on tour of picking up strangers. If we had a spare seat on the bus and a spare ticket to the races I was only too happy to give it away to someone who could use it. I told you about the bookie and the bidet, well this time it was the student and a glass of champagne.

The day before the French Derby my wife and I were having lunch in a busy restaurant when we were joined at our table by a young Australian lad of about 18 or 19 who said he was studying at the Sorbonne. He said he was from Melbourne and our chat soon turned to racing. It turned out he was a follower and knew the form.

He seemed a decent kid so I said he might like to come with us to the Derby. He jumped at the chance and duly presented himself at our hotel the next day for the journey to Chantilly. After the bus is parked the procedure then is that you have to walk through a reserved area to reach the grandstand.

It's very similar to the lawn area in the Members' at Flemington where tables are set up under umbrellas and people can relax with a drink or nibbles. At Chantilly this area is very select—and expensive. As we were passing through one of the ladies noticed Richard Burton sitting at one of the tables. She caught his attention and he came over and posed for photographs, much to everyone's delight.

As we moved on we passed a table which was temporarily deserted by its holders. A glass of champagne caught the eye of our young student, so he picked it up, downed it and walked on. The next minute two gendarmes pounced on us and one put his hand on Frank O'Brien's shoulder. This is the same Frank O'Brien who is the racecourse commentator at Flemington and Moonee Valley and a very good friend of mine.

Not surprisingly Frank was indignant and wanted to know what the gendarme was doing. 'You stole the wine,' the gendarme told him. I had not witnessed the incident but others soon told me it was the young student. I tried to explain this to the gendarmes but to no avail. I needed the kid to own up, but I was told he disappeared once the gendarmes showed up.

The gendarmes wouldn't listen to our protestations of Frank's innocence and led him away to their on-course lock-up. As soon as I could I went to the racecourse administration office and reported the incident. One of the officials accompanied me back to the gendarmes and was able to sort it out with them and Frank was released.

The young bloke who caused the commotion came back and apologised to Frank but said he had run away because he was scared of what might happen to him. We took him back on the bus then said goodbye and I never saw him again.

You would have thought that would have been a lesson to me but, no I was at it again and Chantilly was the racecourse involved. This time though the story is a feel-good one. I had been advised before we left Melbourne that one of the Directors of Southdown Press, which owned *Truth*, would be in Paris, with his wife, on French Derby weekend and he would like to meet with our group.

No problems there, and I thought this would be a good opportunity for a *Truth* Director to learn just how popular these racing tours were. There would be no better introduction than to invite him to join us at the races. There was room on the bus and I always had a couple of spare tickets. So I rang him at his hotel and put the proposition to him. Yes, he and his wife would be delighted to join us.

On the Sunday morning of Derby Day, the couple arrive at our hotel and board our bus for the races. Unfortunately the driver was unfamiliar with Chantilly and parked the bus on the wrong side of the racecourse necessitating a long walk to the grandstand. To my surprise the wife of the Director went to the head of the line, raised her furled umbrella high above her head and called out 'Suivez-moi' (Follow me).

Once she had taken the role of leader, the group got right behind her and took up her shout of 'suivez-moi' turning it into a kind of battle cry, repeating it over and over again. We get to the grandstand and start to study the form for the first race. Suddenly there is a loud shout from one of our party, 'Look, there's a horse in this race called Suivez Moi. We'll have to back it.'

So there is a general exodus to the tote to back Suivez Moi which is showing 50/1. You wouldn't believe it, but it bolts in! There is great cheering and back-slapping for the Director's wife who has become the centre of attention. From then on the success of the day was assured.

I don't know what the Director reported when he got home but it must have been complimentary because the *Truth* Racing Tours continued for nearly 20 years and covered all parts of the globe. They were a great experience for me and I made many friends who enriched my life.

But it wasn't all plain sailing. There were a couple of incidents that caused me no end of worry and I realised that the role of Tour Leader wasn't just a piece of cake. One of them almost deprived the group of seeing the English Derby, which was the whole purpose of their trip.

It happened that this particular year we had a new company handling all the tour arrangements, flights, hotels, land transport, you name it. But there was one job I reserved for myself, handling the Derby tickets.

On our very first trip in 1974 Grenadier Tours had arranged for a marquee to be available for the group during the day, providing lunch and afternoon tea. Very comfortable. But to see the Derby you had to find a place in the grandstand. The trouble was it was packed to the rafters and you would be lucky to see anything except the head and shoulders the guy in front of you.

The crush was so bad that it was also a haven for pickpockets and a couple of our patrons suffered at their tricky hands. I determined that if I ever brought another tour back for the Derby we would have reserved seats so that everyone would get a good view of the race.

Before we left the course that day I mentioned this to the

official who was looking after our group, a lovely lady called Joanne Dillon, who told me there was a small private grandstand adjacent to the main one which allowed groups to reserve a section. This was the Anglesey Stand right opposite the winning post. I said if we ever came back I would write and reserve a block of those seats for our group.

As it turned out we did go back, many times. As I had promised, I would write to Joanne, give her the number of travellers, and she would reserve those seats—at a cost. It was 20 pounds in those first years but had stretched out to 50 pounds by 1985. I would pick up the tickets when we arrived at the course and give her a cheque. No Problems.

By 1985 the world had moved on. So too had Grenadier Travel and we had a new company handling our affairs. I won't dob them in as they were a well-established agency and the itinerary they put together for us was beauty.

When we got down to the details I said I would organise the Derby tickets as I had always done but we needed to add $100 to the price of the tour as the cost of the tickets had gone up.

The Director of the company said there was no need for me to organise the tickets as his agency in London would arrange that. 'They do it every year for us, it's part of our service,' he said. 'You just go to the office the day before the Derby and pick up the tickets.'

I wasn't too happy with this arrangement because I knew how hard those tickets were to get. The Anglesy Stand was booked out months before the Derby was run. I pointed this out to the guy but he assured me the London office had done it all before and had the matter in hand. He was quite insistent so I let it go.

We get to London and on Derby eve I hire a taxi and go to the travel company's office. When I ask for the tickets the guy says,

'Oh, there was a problem there this year and we couldn't get our usual allotment. I've been scouring the black market for you but I've only been able to come up with four tickets.'

'Four tickets for 24 people? you've got to be joking,' I said.

The guy was very apologetic telling me it had never happened before, but four tickets had been the best he could do. My heart sank to my boots. I had 24 people with me who had paid $100 each for those seats. What was I going to tell them?

I got back to our hotel and tried to figure out what to do. I was utterly distressed and couldn't see a way out. My only hope was to give Joanne Dillion a ring at the Jockey Club and see if she had a suggestion.

When I explained the situation to her she said, 'Ron, you are in luck. The leader of an American group rang me an hour ago and said an outbreak of dysentery had gone through their hotel and his people were too ill to come to the races. I have a block of 20 tickets you are welcome to.'

I couldn't believe my ears. A miracle. Of course I immediately accepted her offer. My group numbered 24 so with the four from the Travel Agency we were home and hosed. The only person without a seat was myself but as I had my Press credentials I was able to watch the race from the Press Box.

So while I thoroughly enjoyed my trips around the world as a Tour Leader, it wasn't always beer and skittles. There was a day in Paris when two of our party disappeared from the departure lounge just as we were to board a plane for London. How do you think I felt when we had to take off without them? Fortunately one of our group volunteered to stay behind and find them. He brought them safely to London the following morning much to everyone's relief.

Then there was the day in Ludwigshafen in Germany when our courier gave us the sack. Yes, on this particular tour the travel company provided us with a courier when we departed London for a tour of the Continent. He had charge of the bus and made the decisions where we would go and how long we would stop.

We got offside with him from the start. He was a military man and gave the impression he was the General and we were all like his foot soldiers. His first introduction to us was to hand everyone a list of the optional tours we were expected to take in the various places we were to visit. There was an extra charge for each one.

The first optional tour was the city sights of Amsterdam and the courier said he would be in the town square at 5pm to show us around. No-one turned up. This didn't improve his demeanour towards us as was evident the next day when we headed to Cologne.

When we stopped in Cologne for a one-hour lunch break he said: 'You must be back in one hour otherwise we will go without you,' Well, after an hour three or four of our party hadn't turned. up. 'We go now,' he said to the driver, who started the bus.

'Hold on,' I said, 'we can't go without our friends.'

'We have a timetable to keep, we must go,' the Courier barked.

'There's no way we go without everyone,' I insisted. Those who were on the bus already backed me up, much to the annoyance of the courier. Soon after the others turned up and we were on our way to Koblenz to join a steamer for a cruise along the Rhine.

Imagine our surprise when we found the tour guide on the boat was our courier. No wonder he was in a hurry to leave Cologne. So after a pleasant cruise down the Rhine we pull into Ludwigshafen where our bus is waiting to take us for an overnight at Mannheim. Then it's on for young and old.

Several of the ladies say they need to use the toilet before going any further. This infuriates our courier (I'll call him Johnny) who says: 'Why didn't you use the toilets on the boat?' The ladies reply this was impossible because the toilets were filthy and overflowing.

Fortunately there was a hotel nearby and the ladies made a dash for it. Their toilet break delayed the departure of the bus and this annoyed Johnny even further. He says something like: 'I can't take any more of you Australians. After this, I am finished with you.'

Sure enough when I get up next morning there is no sign of Johnny. The bus and the driver are still there, but what do I do next? The matter is soon solved when I get a call from the tour operator's head office in London confirming that Johnny has left the tour and that a replacement is on his way.

The new chap, a delightful fellow (I'll call him James), arrived that evening and we were off again on schedule the next morning. James was an entirely different person to Johnny and everyone loved him, much to my relief. I realised then that being the Tour Leader you weren't just along for the free ride.

24

Unforgettable Moments

There were many compensations that made those Racing Tours an unforgettable part of my life. Like when I met Gregory Peck at Hollywood Park, and when I got up close and personal with Secretariat and Nijinsky at Claiborne Farm in Kentucky.

Other highlights were discovering the beautiful town of Stressa on the shores of Lake Maggiore in Italy, and visiting the famous Dormello Stud nearby.

There were funny times, difficult times, get-out-of-jail times, and rewarding times. The funniest incident was when we were in America for a day out at the Churchill Downs races. We were booked in for lunch in the posh Secretariat Room at the racecourse and it was an eager group that waited for the bus to take us there.

We were all assembled in the lobby of our hotel, the ladies all dressed up in their finery and the men in their best suits—all except one. As I was checking the numbers I noticed this chap who looked out of place. He was a nice old guy, a pensioner who had saved hard to make the trip. He was remarkable in an unusual way—he had a peg leg.

Due to an accident his left leg had been amputated at the knee and he had been fitted with a wooden replacement. But it wasn't like a conventional leg, it was a peg, just like you would see on some pirates in those old movies. It had no foot.

So Alec is standing there ready to go and looking like something out of the TV series *Hawaiian Five-O*. He has on this loud yellow T-shirt with palm trees all over it and a pair of khaki shorts that came down to his knees. On his right foot he is wearing a sandal.

It was OK for the beach, but hardly the attire for a reserved enclosure at the races. I explained this to Alec and asked him to hurry up and change into more suitable clothes. I don't think he had brought a suit with him but he came back in a respectable jacket and long trousers and a proper black shoe for his right leg.

So we were right to go. There was a cheer for Alec who was very popular with the group. Because of his peg leg he had difficulty getting into the buses and the other men would take it in turns to lift him on. I don't know how Alec would have been received at Churchill Downs in his original outfit but I wasn't taking any chances.

One of the most rewarding things to come out of the tours was the marriage between two of the regular travellers. Each had lost their life-long partner and were travelling alone. On one of our early trips the lady was sitting alone on the bus when the gentleman took the initiative, sat beside her and started a conversation. Simple as that.

They were married the following year and came on several subsequent trips as a married couple. That was our only marriage, but we had a two or three near misses. Romance blossomed while were we away but faded when we returned home.

Another happy outcome concerned a young Irish lad who was working on a stud farm in Italy. After he had shown us around the property and presented the stallions, he mentioned to me that he would love to work in Australia. Did I know of any opportunities for him?

I said I would ask around when I returned home and then write and advise him of the situation. Because of my position as Racing Editor of *Truth* I knew several studmasters. One of them, Alex Katranski, a businessman who had a property at Bacchus Marsh, was interested, and said he would like to know more of the chap's credentials.

I wrote to Willie and gave him Mr. Katranski's address and told him to take it from there. He did, and the result was he came to Australia and took up a position at Mr Katranski's New Underbank stud farm. I've lost track of him as the years have gone on but it is comforting to know that from that Racing Tour in 1975 we were able to help a young chap on his journey through life.

You learn a lot from travelling, and some of the advice you get can turn out to be life saving, well, life preserving, anyway. There was an occasion in Rome on my first trip to Italy in 1974 when my wife and I were walking along a street near the Vatican when we became aware of two nuns coming towards us.

As they drew close they stopped, and one said to my wife: 'You shouldn't wear your handbag over your shoulder like that dear, it is an easy target for the motorbike bandits. They will grab hold of it and you will lose it.'

The nun then demonstrated a safer way. 'You must wrap the strap around the bag then tuck it close against your side and keep to the inside of the pavement if you can,' she said. 'It is very dangerous here now, young thieves sitting behind the driver of the motor bike can grab a strap and whisk your bag away in a flash.'

Lola thanked the ladies and did as she was told. It was good advice and she had no problem with her handbag that year. But the following year we were back in Rome again and Lola still had the same handbag. It was a roomy one and suitable for the little extra things the group might need on the tour.

The handbag also carried our passports and cash, and the group's airways tickets. Each passenger had an individual ticket but for convenience at airports we could check in at the Group Counter. The procedure was I would collect all the tickets and present them in bulk to the airways clerk who would then allocate the seat numbers.

On this occasion we were due to leave Rome for London. To save time I collected all the tickets the evening before and gave them to Lola to keep in her handbag. Normally I would get them locked up in the hotel safe but it was getting late and everyone was anxious to get out for dinner. So off we went.

As we walked along a narrow street I could hear the engine of a motorbike roaring behind us. The next moment it was alongside and the pillion passenger was reaching out towards Lola. As she had learned from the nuns she had her handbag tucked firmly to her side with the strap wrapped around it. She was unaware however that the strap had formed a small loop which was hanging below the main body of the bag.

In a flash the pillion passenger had grabbed the loop and was tugging to pull the bag away. But Lola refused to let go and ran along behind the bike as it was speeding away, still clutching her bag. She must have run 20 or 30 yards over rough cobblestones before a buckle on the bag gave way breaking the grip the thief had on it.

With the tension broken Lola crashed to the roadway and the thief sped away empty handed. When the rest of us caught up we found Lola dazed and bleeding. We got her into the doorway of a nearby building and examined her wounds—skin off her elbows and knees which had caused bleeding but nothing serious, she was just badly shaken.

As she hobbled back to the hotel she gave me a wry smile and said proudly: 'But they couldn't get my handbag.'

It wasn't until the next morning that we realised how serious the loss of the handbag would have been. Not only did it contain the London-bound tickets for the group but our money and passports as well. Losing them would have been a disaster.

When we both contemplated the incident later we recalled the meeting with the two nuns the year before. 'If it had not been for those two women,' Lola said, 'I would have been carrying that bag slung over my shoulder and it would have been gone.'

25

What A Coincidence

Have you noticed when travelling overseas how sometimes you meet someone from home and you think, 'fancy seeing you, what a coincidence'? Well there was a coincidence on our English Derby Tour in 1975 that takes some beating. Before we left Melbourne Lola and I were having dinner one evening with her mother and discussing our forthcoming trip.

'So you are going to Paris,' says Lola's mum. 'Well, you know my neighbour's daughter Helen, well, she will be in Paris about the same time. You might run into her.'

'Yes, mum, we might, but Paris is an awfully big place,' says Lola.

Our tour takes us to the Hotel Chaplain, a nice comfortable Parisian hotel close to the Gare du Nord and our kick-off place for a visit to the French Derby. On Derby morning we put on our best race gear and leave the room to catch the bus to Chantilly. As we step into the passage the door of the room next door opens. And who walks out but… Helen!

We did visit some fantastic places on those tours and one of the most beautiful was Stressa on the shores of Lake Maggiore in northern Italy. It was memorable for several reasons not the least of which was the Hotel in which our group stayed. It was called the Regina Palace and was the most luxurious of all the hotels in which our groups stayed over almost 20 years.

The area is steeped in history and we were lucky enough to have a guide who took us to an island just off-shore where Napoleon spent some time with Josephine. A highlight of that tour was a boat trip up Lake Maggiore to Luino where we picked up a bus that took us for the short trip into Switzerland to the town of Lugano. We returned to Stressa via Como to complete a memorable day out.

This book is not meant to be a travel guide but I mention some of the fabulous places we went to on the Racing Tours because if you do take a trip overseas a visit to the places I have mentioned will only add to your enjoyment.

The town of Stressa was so memorable for me, not only because of its beauty, but because it was so close to the Dormello Stud founded by the breeding wizard Federico Tessio. This was where Tessio bred his unbeaten champions Ribot and Nearco, two stallions that have left an indelible mark on the thoroughbred breeding industry throughout the world.

Dormello runs alongside Lake Maggiore and some of the paddocks for broodmares and their foals run right down to the water, an idyllic setting for producing racing champions. This was where Tessio's broodmare Ada Hunter roamed before he sold her to David Hains, one of Melbourne's leading breeders in the latter part of the 20th century.

I knew David very well during that period. He was racing so many good horses I was constantly ringing him for information about their progress and reporting on their racetrack deeds. Among the stars of David's team at that time were Kingston Town, Rose of Kingston, Spirit of Kingston and Kingston Rule, who won the 1990 Melbourne Cup.

David put his Dormello mare Ada Hunter to the freakish

sprinter Bletchingly to produce the champion Kingston Town, who won three consecutive W.S. Cox Plates, and was the one of the inaugural inductees into. Australia's Racing Hall of Fame.

The connection between David Hains and Dormello is rather remarkable. It came about through his association with golfing legend Norman von Nida, who was a racing tragic. When David was setting up his Kingston Park Stud in the late 1950s he asked Norman to select some broodmares for him.

Through his international golfing experiences Norman knew of the reputation of Dormello and made the famous Italian stud the source of his mission.

He bought six broodmares from Dormello, among them Ada Hunter, who was a granddaughter of Tessio's unbeaten champion Ribot. A few years later Tessio also sold his Italian Derby winning stallion Claude to David, who installed him at Kingston Park, situated at Merricks North in Victoria.

David had a very good mare Kingston Rose who had won six races before he decided to retire her. He put her to Claude and the resulting foal was named Rose of Kingston. She was a champion. Among her victories were the AJC Oaks, and the AJC Derby, a race no filly had won in the previous 38 years.

When Rose of Kingston retired David continued his connection with Dormello by sending her to America to be mated with the Triple Crown winner Secretariat, a great-grandson of Dormello's unbeaten Nearco.

The choice of Secretariat as Rose of Kingston's consort was not surprising. He retired to stud with a reputation as the world's best racehorse!

Whether he deserved such high praise, who can tell? But there was certainly evidence to give it credence. It needed an almighty galloper to earn such praise and Secretariat was indeed such a horse.

When he won America's Triple Crown—the Kentucky Derby, The Preakness and the Belmont Stakes—in 1973, he became the first horse to do so in 25 years, and he ran record times in each of those three races.

His success in the Belmont Stakes, which he won by an astounding 31 lengths, was one of the most sensational victories of all time.

I mentioned that I got up close and personal with Secretariat on a Racing Tour visit to Claiborne and that is literally true. He was the most docile of stallions, posing patiently for photos with members of our group and letting them stroke his neck and rub his muzzle.

His coupling with Rose of Kingston was designed to produce a champion. It didn't, but it did result in an outstanding stayer called Kingston Rule, one of the most beautiful horses I have ever seen. He was tall and handsome with a clear and penetrating eye. His satin-like chestnut coat shone like burnished bronze in the sunlight. When I saw Secretariat he was past his prime, but they say Kingston Rule was a 'ringer' for his dad.

Kingston Rule didn't achieve the great heights you would expect of his breeding, but he did win the Melbourne Cup of 1990 and in doing so he ran a record time of 3 minutes 16.3 seconds for the 3200 metres, which still stands.

26

Shades Of The Golden Slipper

I told you of the amazing coincidence of meeting a neighbour in Paris on one of *Truth*'s Racing Tours, well, another remarkable occurrence took place in Amsterdam on one our subsequent tours.

As it often happened after we booked into our hotel the group would ask me where we were going for dinner. I was usually as ignorant as they were, but on this occasion I was prepared. Before we left Australia a friend had recommended a restaurant in Amsterdam he said we would like.

So I rounded everyone up and we set off to walk to the eatery, which was a good hit-out from our hotel. Unfortunately, when we arrived we were told this was a special occasion and the restaurant was booked out. I was embarrassed. I had brought all these people this long way and now I was stranded with them in a city I knew little about.

The only thing to do was to walk on and hope we could find a place that could accommodate us. We did see a few restaurants but I didn't like the look of them so we pressed on hoping something would turn up. It did. Ahead of us was a brightly lit restaurant with an inviting window display. I told the group to hang on while I checked to see if they could take us.

As I stood at the reception counter I saw on the wall opposite the picture of a horse galloping at full stretch that looked strangely familiar. When the receptionist came up I asked if she could tell me the name of the horse.

'That's a picture of Roy Higgins riding Storm Queen at trackwork at Flemington,' she said. You could have bowled me over with a feather. What was a photo of Storm Queen doing here in a restaurant in Amsterdam half a world from Melbourne?

'Roy Higgins gave it to my sister Akke Van Den Dolden,' the lady explained. 'She was strapping Storm Queen for Bart Cummings.' The lady then introduced herself as Nellie, and said she was the owner of the restaurant together with her husband Martin. 'You would be very welcome here,' she said. 'We will make room for your party.'

It turned out be one of the best nights of our tour with Nellie and Martin joining in, blowing up balloons and throwing streamers around to give it a real party atmosphere. Everyone loved it and what looked like being a disaster of an evening turned into a raging success.

I was able to tell Nellie that I knew her sister Akke very well and that she was one of the most highly regarded strappers in Melbourne. She had worked with such top trainers as Angus Armanasco, Colin Hayes and Tommy Smith before linking up with Bart.

Akke always stood out when she was leading a horse in the mounting yard because of her immaculate attire of jodhpurs, white shirt and navy jacket or jumper. I would often chat with her at trackwork and learned that her father was a pilot in the Indonesian Air Force and was stationed in Australia when World War II broke out.

When the Japanese occupied Indonesia Akke and her mother spent four years in a concentration camp. She didn't see her father again until he returned to Indonesia at the end of the war.

Akke told me that after a few years back in Indonesia her father decided to take his family to Holland where both he and his wife had relatives. But after the Hungarian Revolution in 1956 her father feared there would be another war and made the decision to resettle in Australia.

I am able to tell you all this because I did an in-depth interview with Akke for *Truth* that told the full story of her life and her love of horses. That's why I found it so remarkable that I should find a photo of Storm Queen, the horse she strapped to win the Golden Slipper in 1966, hanging on the wall of a restaurant I had no intention of visiting in faraway Amsterdam.

Akke Van den Dooren, strapper for Bart Cummings and sister of Nellie, restaurant owner in Amsterdam.

27

Dramas With Big Philou

One of the most tragic things I ever saw on a racecourse was the sight of Big Philou standing in his stall at Flemington on Melbourne Cup Day in 1969, head bowed, hardly able to stand up, and the wall behind him covered top to bottom with his excrement.

A few minutes before, the warning siren had sounded announcing that Big Philou had been withdrawn from the race. No wonder, the horse was a sick and sorry sight. The announcement came as a complete shock to everyone, including his trainer Bart Cummings who stood in front of the horse's stall totally bemused at the sudden turn of events.

Big Philou was equal favourite at 4/1 and his scratching led to a an investigation which lasted more than a year before it was resolved—not to everyone's liking, but at least justice was done.

After Big Philou was treated by veterinary surgeons on-course he was slowly walked back to Cummings' stables where further tests were carried out. It took two weeks for the results to come through. They proved what many people believed, that the horse had been doped.

The drug was a laxative named Danthron which had led to the horse scouring uncontrollably. It was a cruel thing to do to a defenceless animal. Stewards and the police questioned several people including Cummings' staff without success, until a breakthrough came about five months later.

A former member of Bart's staff, Leslie Lewis, who had defected to New Zealand, was extradited back to Australia and charged with doping Big Philou. Unfortunately not enough evidence could be gathered to show he did the deed. Instead, he was outed for having doped another of Cummings' horses, King Pedro, a charge which was proven.

The Law jailed Lewis for six months and the VRC stewards disqualified him for life. However, the story of Les Lewis didn't end there for me. Sometime after his release from jail I was instrumental in helping him get back on his feet—for a while.

Looking back now after 50 years I wonder how I could have done that, knowing what he had done to Big Philou and what a crook he was? But I didn't know that when I had first met him some years before.

In those days, from the 1960s to the '90s, I was a regular track watcher at Flemington. I would be there three or four mornings a week, often in the dark in winter, and before sun-up in summer. I got to know the trainers, their foremen, the strappers and the stable hands. It was a little community down there with lots of racing talk, gossip, a bit of banter, and a coffee in the canteen to top the morning off.

One of the stablehands I would chat with was Les Lewis who was working for Bart and would bring his horses to the track and see them safely home again. He was a talkative fellow and a good source of snippets for the paper.

After he was pinched for the King Pedro job however, everyone knew he was the man behind the Big Philou doping and everyone dropped off him.

A few years later I was walking past the Gill Memorial

Home, a Salvation Army Hostel for homeless men in A'Beckett Street, which is adjacent to La Trobe Street where *Truth* had its offices. You had to walk past the Gill to get to the Sabloniere Hotel which was the watering hole for the *Truth* staff.

On one of my excursions I noticed a fellow sitting on the pavement and slumped against the wall of the building. It was Lewis. I must have said something like 'What are you doing here, Les?' because he told me he was waiting to get a bed for the night.

I must have felt sorry for him to see him like that, because, after all, he had been a help to me when I was writing stories from the track. So I told him I would see what I could do for him. I mentioned his situation to a friend of mine, Bill Moon, who owned the Union Hotel at Ascot Vale. Bill said he was about to open a new bar at his hotel and would require a new barman.

Les goes to see Bill and gets the job. I used to go to the Union Hotel often, a lot of racing people drank there and it was a good source of information. After two or three weeks I asked Bill: 'How's Les going?'

'He's gone,' replied Bill. 'I found him tickling the peter (robbing the till) and had to sack him.'

I lost contact with Les after that but his name did bob up in the *Sun News Pictorial* many years later when he confessed to doping Big Philou. He said he was dying of cancer and wanted to clear his conscience.

Les has since passed away and all I can say is that while he never did me any harm, he did hurt a lot of other people. His doping of Big Philou was a dastardly deed that affected not only the poor horse but could have caused a horrible accident had he taken his place in the field.

28

Dulcify Was A Tragic Loss

A horse breaking down during a race is one of the most pathetic sights you can see on a racecourse. It doesn't happen often, and when it does it leaves a lasting memory. So I will never forget the day Dulcify broke down in the Melbourne Cup of 1979.

Dulcify was one of the most popular horses in Australia and his followers had sent him out a 3/1 favourite in that fateful Melbourne Cup. Half a mile from home he appeared to be beautifully placed, a couple off the rails and tucked in behind the leaders. He was perfectly poised for a clear run down the straight.

But what we couldn't see from the Press Box was that Dulcify was in dire straits. He had been galloped on by Hyperno about a mile from home and was running on empty. It wasn't until just before the turn into the straight that his jockey Brent Thompson realised something was badly amiss and began to pull him up.

Hyperno went on to win the race while racecourse attendants were preparing to rush out a screen to hide the faltering Dulcify from the public's gaze. Up in the Press seats we thought the horse was going to be put down, but soon afterwards the horse ambulance arrived and Dulcify was taken away.

What happened after that is a bit murky. My recall of it was that Dulcify was taken to Colin Hayes' stable in Fisher Parade which was adjacent to the racecourse and he was examined there by Colin's vet, Campbell Baker. I did speak to Campbell later and he told me that when he did a rectal examination he could feel pieces of shattered bone in the rectal canal. 'That confirmed the hopelessness of the situation,' he said.

Campbell was still emotional when he spoke to me. Looking back over my notes of that conversation I get an eerie feeling of how tragic the occasion must have been for him. He had said: 'That day will never go out of my mind, even the next day, it was an amazing feeling. When I saw him, the fractures were so complete, very uncomfortable. He had no support and was getting muscle spasms. The decision (to put him down) was not difficult.'

It was after Dulcify had been euthanised that speculation began as to the whereabouts of his carcass. There was one report that it had been taken to the Saleyards nearby and dumped in a pen next to a dead sheep. There was another story that he had been taken to a local knackery.

But the most widely circulated story was that he had been taken away and buried under a big tree on a country property. That's the story I heard from Colin Hayes' trusted lieutenant, Ron Nestor. When I asked Ron the whereabouts of the tree he said he couldn't tell me. I think I got the message. I have never seen Dulcify's grave and I don't know anyone who has.

My recollection of Dulcify doesn't end there. I was reminded of him when I went to Belmont racecourse in New York and saw a small statue of Secretariat taking pride of place in front of one of the grandstands. By small, I mean it wasn't life-size like Makybe Diva at Flemington.

Belmont was the place where Secretariat ran one of the greatest races in history winning the Belmont Stakes by 31 lengths. I thought how fitting he should be honoured at the track where he had raced with such distinction. Then I thought of Dulcify, struck down at Flemington before he could complete what promised to be one of the most stunning careers on the Australian turf.

When I returned to Melbourne, I suggested in *Truth* that the VRC should erect a statue of Dulcify, similar to that of Secretariat, on the lawns at Flemington. I wrote that Dulcify was the most popular horse in Australia, yet we had nothing tangible by which to remember him.

You could say his win in the 1979 W.S. Cox Plate by seven lengths was testimony enough to keep his memory alive forever, but to me that wasn't enough. Dulcify was favourite for the Melbourne Cup when he was fatally injured trying desperately to win for the punters who had supported him. When his tragic death was announced it threw a pall over the racecourse.

My opinion then was, and still is today, that Flemington was the right place to have a permanent reminder of this wonderful horse who had never been beaten on that racecourse. Dulcify had five starts at Flemington and won them all, three Group 1's, the Victoria Derby, Australian Cup, and LKS Mackinnon Stakes and two Group 2 races the Craiglee Stakes, and Turnbull Stakes. And he hadn't long turned four!

The VRC committee didn't pick up on my suggestion, and that's fair enough. They obviously had their reasons. But times have changed in the past 40 years and the VRC has erected four statues in that period, Phar Lap (the greatest), Makybe Diva (three Melbourne Cups), Roy Higgins (11 Victorian Jockey Premierships) and Bart Cummings (12 Melbourne Cups), all thoroughly deserved.

Maybe I'm just an old sentimentalist but, perhaps one day, the VRC will find a little spot for Dulcify so that his many admirers will find a place to pay him their respects.

29

George Moore Was The Best

I have been very fortunate to have met so many fine people in the racing industry, and luckier still to call them friends. Some I got to know very well and others, like George Moore, not very well at all. I didn't see much of George because he was based in Sydney but nonetheless I will always regard him as a friend, as well as being Australia's finest jockey.

Although I was rarely in his company there was one memorable occasion when we became quite close. It happened in Tokyo in 1969 when George was invited to ride in an Invitational jockey's race and I was there to cover the Eighth Asian Racing Conference.

While I was acting as a reporter for Rupert Murdoch's newspapers I was also listed as an official delegate to the conference. This credential allowed me to be part of all official meetings and functions and ensured the VRC's submissions got good coverage back in Melbourne.

So I was wearing my reporter's hat on the Friday morning before Sunday's race when I was invited to join an official party for an inspection of Fuchu Racecourse, where the big event was to be held. Luckily, I was allocated to share a limousine with George Moore and his young son Gary.

Because of recent heavy snow in Tokyo the Invitatational

race had been transferred from the course proper to an inside track composed of sand and gravel. When we got out of the car and had a look, George turned to me and said: 'I won't ride on that. I came here to ride on grass, not on metal.'

The track wasn't a pretty sight. Trucks were clearing the snow and there were pools of water everywhere. 'I can't ride on that track,' I remember George saying. 'The horses will kick up the gravel and I can't risk any damage to my eyes. I haven't ridden on dirt or sand since 1944, except for one trip to America.'

I was furiously taking notes. This was a big story. The Japanese Racing Association had heavily promoted the Invitational race on the strength of George Moore and the leading New Zealand rider, Bill Skelton, participating and here was George saying he wouldn't ride.

George was pretty stirred up, telling me he hadn't ridden at Albion Park in Queensland for the past 10 years because the sand there had caused so much damage to his eyes that he had to have two skin growths removed.

Of course, while we were speaking the Japanese officials were standing close by wondering what was going on. Then George asked me to inform them that he would not ride. I clearly remember the look of consternation on the face of the fellow I spoke to, a friendly chap called Akiro Kondo, whom I had got to know. He couldn't believe what I was telling him, but he quickly relayed the message to his superiors.

George was told that he had until 11 o'clock the following morning (Saturday) to give official notice that he would not ride. Before we left the racecourse George said he wanted to have a look at the grandstand so we walked inside and George said he thought it was fantastic.

George's 17-year-old apprentice jockey son Gary, who had

joined his mother and father on this trip, had broken his shoulder in a recent fall and was currently on the sidelines. He was an exuberant young fellow who took great delight running through the corridors of the grandstand and skidding along on the highly polished floors.

Before we left Fuchu Gary turned to his father and said: 'I would ride for you dad, but I can't because of this shoulder. I would ride on any course.' I thought that typified Gary's nature, a well-mannered kid, full of life and fun, and loyal to his father. Later events in Gary's career endorsed that view, as you will read.

The Japanese officials were in a flap. George had thrown a spanner in the works and it had to be sorted out. When the deadline expired on Saturday morning and George had not changed his mind the JRA called a press conference. The Press Liaison Officer, Masao Tomita, said he had called George that morning and was told twice he would not ride on the dirt track and there was no alternative but to replace him.

But that wasn't the end of it. Come Saturday afternoon George decides to go back to Fuchu to have a look at the minor meeting that is being held there. He watches the last three races and decides the dirt track had dried out so well that he would be prepared to ride on it.

So he asks me to convey his decision to the Japanese officials. This only further confuses them because they have already substituted a rider in George's place.

On returning to the hotel George asks Brian Crowley, head of the Sydney delegation, to see if he could have him reinstated. Mr. Crowley puts George's case to the Japanese but they say there is nothing they can do about it as the Press, radio and television have all been notified about the change of rider.

That evening George invites me to dinner with him, his

wife Iris, and Gary. During the meal, and over a glass of rose wine, George explained why he was so concerned about the state of the dirt track. He had already told me of the damage sand had caused to his eyes, but he also had other concerns.

He pointed out that he had no insurance in Japan and was worried about what might happen if something went wrong. At the back of his mind was the fact he was booked to ride the flying Sydney filly Special Girl in the Golden Slipper a week later, and he considered her a certainty.

'Special Girl is the greatest,' he told me. 'She is the equal of Todman, and I saw plenty of him when I was riding Tulloch. The first day I rode her I came home and said "I've just ridden the best two-year-old ever".'

That day was 2 October the previous year, when Special Girl won her first start, the Tiny Tots Stakes at Canterbury by 10 lengths starting at 14/1 on and running a race record. Special Girl had two more starts before the Slipper, coming back on 2 February to win over six furlongs at Rosehill, again starting at 14/1 on, and winning by 10 lengths.

At her final start before the Slipper she won again, this time beating the Widden Stakes winner Celina over six furlongs at Warwick Farm. She started at 10/1 on but scored by only three-quarters of a lengths because Moore eased her down at the finish, earning a reprimand from the stewards.

These victories set the stage for Special Girl's clash with Victoria's best two-year-old Vain, who was unbeaten in four starts in Melbourne. Vain was being dubbed a super colt after this impressive string of victories which included an eight-lengths romp in the Maribyrnong Plate up the straight at Flemington.

The pair were set to meet in the Golden Slipper which was to be Vain's next start, two weeks after he had won the Sires' Produce

Stakes at Flemington starting at 9/2, strolling in by four lengths.

With both Vain and Special Girl unbeaten, the rivalry between Sydney and Melbourne became intense. The newspapers in both cities were playing up the race as one of the most enthralling clashes between two-year-olds in years.

But George had no doubt about the result. 'She'll win by five lengths,' he told me that night in Japan. 'Vain has to give her 7lb (3kg). She could give him 5lb!'

He went on to say: 'I said Tulloch was the best horse I've ridden, and I was right. But she is the best I've ridden (since), and that includes the best in England. No matter where she draws nothing will head her.'

Vain (4/1) left from barrier four like a bullet. Special Girl was also fast away from barrier 10, but not as fast as Vain, and despite Moore's urgings she could not get on terms. At the halfway mark she was at his flanks but the further they went the further Vain drew ahead. Towards the finish Special Girl, the 13/8 on favourite, had had enough and faded to finish fifth.

That's how good a horse Vain was, he beat the unbeatable. So you shouldn't be surprised that I rate him more highly than Black Caviar, the modern sprinting sensation who was unbeaten in 25 starts from 2008 to 2013.

George Moore told me many stories s during that memorable dinner in Tokyo often referring to his humble beginnings. He told me how he grew up in a grass hut with a mud floor at Mackay in Queensland adding: 'I had a more humble beginning than Lionel Rose,' he said. (Lionel Rose, who won the world bantamweight boxing championship in Tokyo in 1968, grew up in the poor aboriginal settlement of Jackson's Creek in Victoria.)

He also re-told a famous story of how Tommy Smith

predicted he would train a Derby winner and George would ride it. 'We were both at Caulfield, I was a 16-year-old apprentice and Tommy was there strapping horses. We used to race each other on the steeplechase track. He would say to me: "I'll be the top trainer and you'll be the leading jockey. You'll win a Derby for me".'

Tommy got his trainers' licence two years later in 1941 and in 1949 at Randwick, George made that prophesy a reality by winning the AJC Derby on the 100/1 shot Playboy, trained by Smith.

I wrote earlier that I would have more to say about Gary Moore because what George told me in Tokyo turned out to be so prophetic. George said how much he wanted Gary to succeed as a jockey.

'I want Gary to be the leading jockey,' he told me. 'That's my greatest ambition. I would have retired if it hadn't been for him. I want to see him get a start.'

Gary fulfilled George's wishes big time. He won seven Hong Kong jockey premierships, and one French. Among his most important wins was the 1981 Prix de l'Arc de Triomphe on Gold River. He was also successful in England where he won the 1988 Classic, the 1000 Guineas, on Ravinella.

Gary went on to become the leading trainer in Macau, winning the Premiership eight times. He is now training in Sydney where he is building up a successful business.

But the Moore saga didn't end with that dinner at the New Otani Hotel. The following day was the big Invitational race at Fuchu and I was there with the Australian delegation to watch it. In the meantime George flew out with his family to Hong Kong, en route to Sydney. When I returned to the hotel after the races a surprise was waiting for me.

I found an envelope had been slipped under the door. It

was a letter from George. In it he thanked me for my friendship and company while we had been together in Tokyo. He also expressed his disappointment at the way he felt he had been treated by the Sydney delegation.

George was hurt that he and his family had not been invited to join in parties with other members of the AJC group. He felt he had been left out in the cold. He ended the letter saying he felt he had been treated like a second-class citizen.

It was pretty strong stuff, the leading jockey criticising members of the body that was controlling racing in Sydney. It would make a big story if it hit the papers. I was there in Tokyo working for the Murdoch chain and one of those papers was the Sydney *Daily Mirror*. What was I to do?

Was George's letter a personal one to me, or was he telling me he wanted his side of the story told?

The deadline for the *Daily Mirror* was 9am Tokyo time the following morning. I wrestled with the situation overnight and came up with the answer: George would not have gone to all the trouble to relate the events in such detail in a letter unless he meant me to use it.

I wasn't sure, but that was my gut feeling. I just hoped I was right. So I filed a story to the *Mirror* highlighting that George felt he had been treated like a second-class citizen.

The story made front page news. The repercussions began soon after the Sydney delegation got home. George was summoned to appear before the committee of the Australian Jockey Club for his failure to carry out his riding engagement in Japan.

George wrote a letter of apology to the committee and enclosed a cheque for $1,106.90, the cost of his airfare which had been paid by the AJC. The hearing lasted only 15 minutes with Moore being directed to write a letter of apology to the Japan Racing Association.

George's stand in Tokyo however was vindicated after the running of the big race without him. Bill Skelton, who was representing New Zealand, said his mount, which ran unplaced, had been hit by the metal which was mixed with the sandy surface.

There was also an article in the Japanese sporting paper *Hochi Shimbun* defending George. It said: 'It is only natural for a foreign jockey, who always respects a contract, to have refused to ride in a race if the track was changed at the last minute.'

George retired two years after the Tokyo incident and I never got close enough to him again to reminisce about those days in Japan. George went to France where he trained for a short time, then took up residence in Hong Kong where he trained for 13 years winning 11 premierships.

I had always wanted to meet up with George again to ask him how he felt when I released some of the contents of his letter to the *Daily Mirror*. Did I do the right thing or not? The opportunity came 32 years later in 2001 in Melbourne. George had just been inducted into the Australian Racing Hall of Fame and I was on the selection committee.

There was a lavish dinner to present the inaugural awards and, as a member of the selection panel, I was invited to share pre-dinner drinks with the winners in a private room. I saw George standing a few paces away and he looked across and smiled.

As I moved forward to shake his hand an attendant took his arm and led him away to the official table. The opportunity was gone and I didn't see George again. He died on 9 January 2008. But that brief smile across a crowded room said it all.

30

Roy Higgins Was A Gentleman

Roy Higgins, the champion Victorian jockey of the 1960s and '70s, was one of the most decent human beings I ever met. I had a great working relationship with Roy and was constantly in touch with him because he was always making news. I could ring him at any time and he would always take my call. And he was the same with all the journalists.

Roy never let his success go to his head. He was just as comfortable talking to Joe Blow the punter as he was with the Queen of England, as he did on a couple of occasions. So you can imagine how I felt for him when he had a 'bust up' with legendary trainer Bart Cummings.

Roy and Bart were one of the most successful jockey-trainer partnerships in the history of Australian racing. They won everything together over almost 20 years, Melbourne Cups, Golden Slippers, Newmarket Handicaps, Derbies and Oaks, and so many others.

It had been an amazing ride for Roy. He was a kid who grew up in Deniliquin, the son of poor parents (Roy's words), undersized for his age, and with little education. In one of our many interviews he told me that racing was 'his gateway to life'.

'What was a little, uneducated runt like me, going to do?' he asked.

'I was 14, five foot one (153cm), basically uneducated, and living in a small country town. Where was I going in life? People would keep saying to you, "Hey, you would make a good jockey". They didn't say you would make a good footballer, or a good Prime Minister. Instead they would say, "You have got the right size to be a jockey".'

Roy remembered being kicked out of school at 14 because he used to play the wag and go and hide all day in the horse stalls at Jimmy Watters' stables, which were next door. It seemed only natural that he would become apprenticed to Watters.

'In my day 99% of jockeys were uneducated,' he said. 'You left school at 14 and were riding at 15.'

I think that is why I admired Roy so much. To come from such a humble beginning and ride for kings and queens and become a household name among the racing people of Australia took guts and determination. And he did it all himself. He even taught himself the art of public speaking.

'I worked very hard at improving myself, and I used to watch and follow and study,' he recalled. 'I used Bill Williamson as a guide. He was the best rider I ever saw. I would watch him, not only when he was riding, but off the horse as well, like in the jockeys' room and the mounting yard. I just tried learning from others.'

Roy's blossoming record as a jockey wasn't lost on the champion trainer Bart Cummings who recognised his talent and soon began to put him on. They became a formidable pair and their partnership ran a relatively smooth path until one fateful day at Flemington in 1980.

It was a summer's morning, a Thursday, two or three weeks before the running of the Blue Diamond Stakes. I was there as usual, shortly before dawn, to watch the track gallops before heading to the office. Bart was out in the centre of the course, close to the trainers' stand, putting his team through their paces.

Roy and Harry White were doing the riding, everything was calm and normal. I was standing not far from Bart waiting for an opportunity to speak to him.

But in a few minutes the scene had changed and the serenity of the morning was shattered by an event that led to one of the saddest sights I have seen on a racecourse.

Roy rode up on Ming Dynasty, stopping by Bart to get his instructions. As he did so he noticed Harry going out to gallop the two-year-old filly Silver Shoes. He called out to Harry to wait while he spoke to Bart. I wasn't privy to the conversation, but the next thing I see, Roy jumps off Ming Dynasty and throws the reins straight at Bart, collecting him on the head.

I don't remember Roy's exact words but it sounded like: 'That's it, I'm finished, I'll never ride for you again.' He then stormed off towards the trainers' stand, sat down on a piece of concrete underneath it and poured himself a cup of coffee from a thermos he had placed their previously, as was his habit.

As I walked towards Roy to find out what had happened, I could see that he was visibly upset. He was shaking and crying. He looked so sad I felt I had to do something. I tried to calm him down with words like: 'Don't worry, it'll be OK. Just take it easy.' But Roy wouldn't be soothed. 'I'll never ride for him again,' he repeated.

And Roy never did. I found out from Bart later that Roy expected to be riding Silver Shoes at Flemington on the Saturday and got upset when Bart told him Harry White would ride her. Roy was the stable's No.1 rider and expected to be on the horses that were in his weight range.

But Bart had decided he wanted the same jockey to ride the filly in Saturday's race and in the Blue Diamond. 'You can't ride her in the Blue Diamond because she hasn't got your weight,' he had explained to Roy. But this didn't cut any ice with Roy and it set off his outburst.

Roy retired from riding three years later and, true to his word, he didn't ride for Bart again. But they did patch up their relationship before he quit. As Bart explained in his book *BART, My Life*: 'We had too many good memories in common.'

I had many friends among the jockeys, some I saw more often than others. Two in particular who lived close by were Midge Didham and Harry White. As well as being jockeys, and therefore part of my working world, they were mates as well. Midge, whose actual name was Earnest, came over from New Zealand to ride for Tony Lopes and, as I was a regular visitor to that stable, I got to know Midge quite well.

One night I invited him and his wife Doreen to dinner at the new home my wife Lola and I had built at Keilor, and they liked the design of the house so much Midge asked if I would lend him the plans as he was about to build a new home himself.

I had no objection, so Midge was able to incorporate some of the features into his own ideas. Somehow the fact we both had similar houses brought us closer together, and we are still good mates today.

Harry White didn't live far away in Park Street in Essendon and every Thursday afternoon I would drop off a copy of *Truth* in his mailbox on my way home. *Truth* was always the first paper out with acceptances for Saturday's races and it gave Harry a bit of a heads up if he got his copy before anyone else.

Harry was a member of the Northern Golf Club in Glenroy and I would occasionally go there to have a hit. One day Harry and I teamed up for a round and the conversation was, naturally, about racing. Harry opened up that he'd been hurt by the criticism

Ron and Lola join hands to enter *The Guinness Book of World Records* for the longest human circle in the world in Lucca, Italy.
Right: Lola's number for the record.

Truth co-owner Mark Day presents Ron with his retirement portrait, painted by John Howley in 1993.

Colin Hayes with his trainer sons Peter (right) and David.

Truth co-owner Owen Thompson amuses Ron and wife Lola at Ron's retirement dinner.

Nellie (nee Van den Dooren) and husband Martin (holding picture of Storm Queen) at their restaurant in Amsterdam.

Ted Humphrey (dark suit) and Frank Sedgeman (right) with some of Ted's troupe of international tennis stars.

Lola plays ball with Keeka and Ginger Mick in the garden of the villa in Tuscany.

Ron's retirement villa in Tuscany.

Right: Town of Grosio in Northern Italy where Ron's grandfather was born.

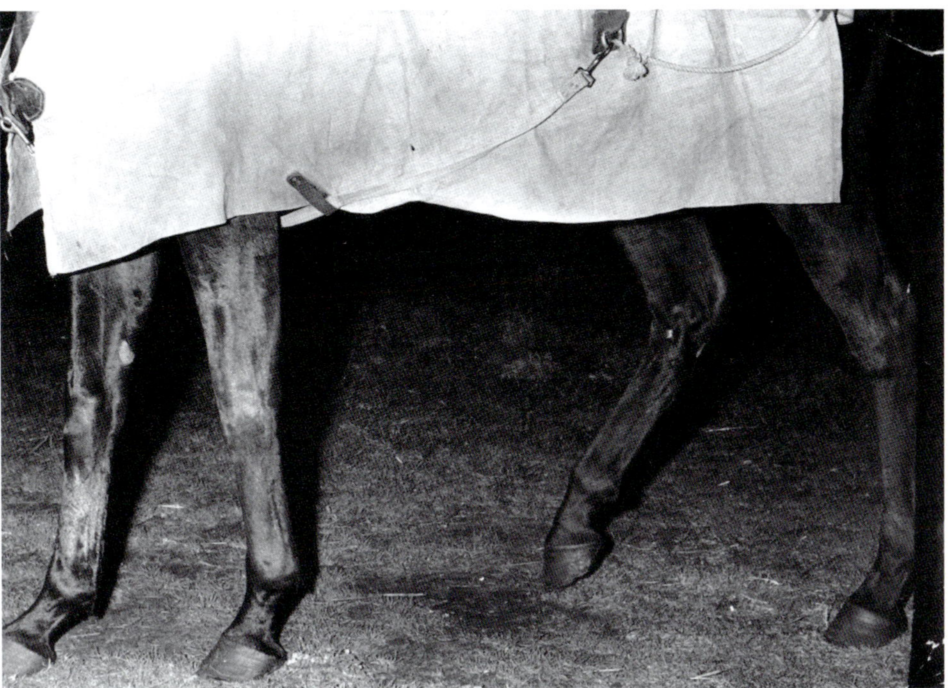

The tell-tale chestnut on the inside of Regal Vista's foreleg.

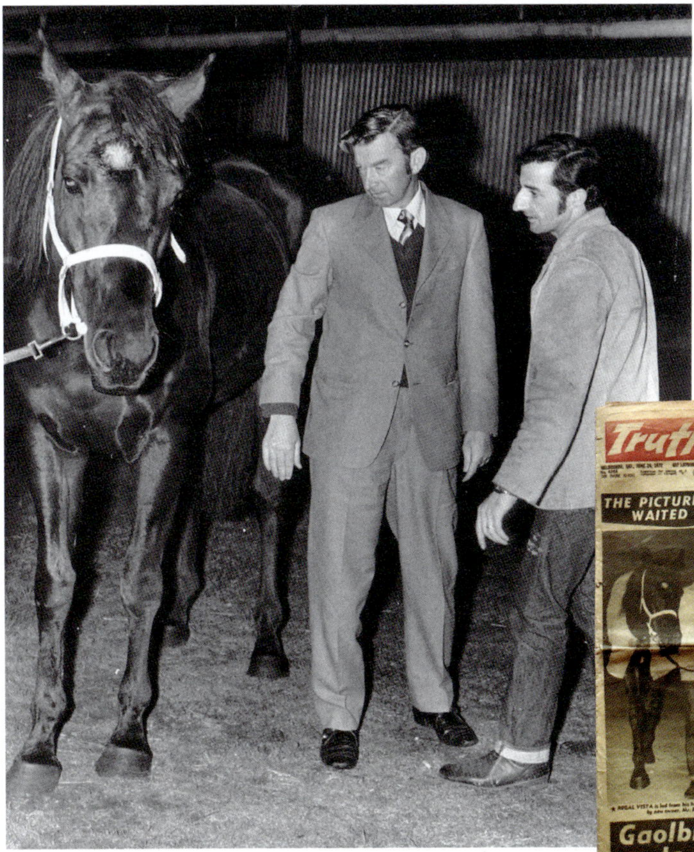

Ron checks out Regal Vista's brands with Rick Renzella at hideaway in Cranbourne.

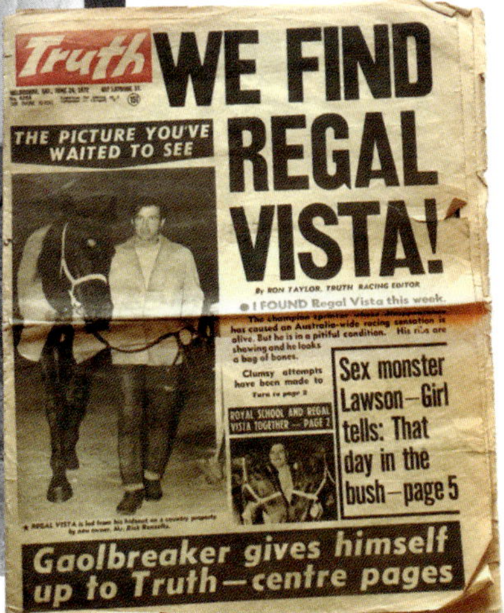

Truth

WE FIND REGAL VISTA!

THE PICTURE YOU'VE WAITED TO SEE

By RON TAYLOR, TRUTH RACING EDITOR

● I FOUND Regal Vista this week.

The champion sprinter whose disappearance has caused an Australia-wide racing sensation is alive. But he is in a pitiful condition. His ribs are showing and he looks a bag of bones.

Clumsy attempts have been made to

Turn to page 2

★ REGAL VISTA is led from his hideout on a country property by new owner, Mr. Rick Renzella.

ROYAL SCHOOL AND REGAL VISTA TOGETHER — PAGE 2

Sex monster Lawson—Girl tells: That day in the bush—page 5

Gaolbreaker gives himself up to Truth—centre pages

Ron discussing prospects with Andrew Peacock at Moonee Valley. Note Andrew's daughter Jane listening in.

Ron commentating for Channel 10.

Ron interviewing Lord before his memorable clash with Tulloch in the Queens' Cup at Flemington in 1960.

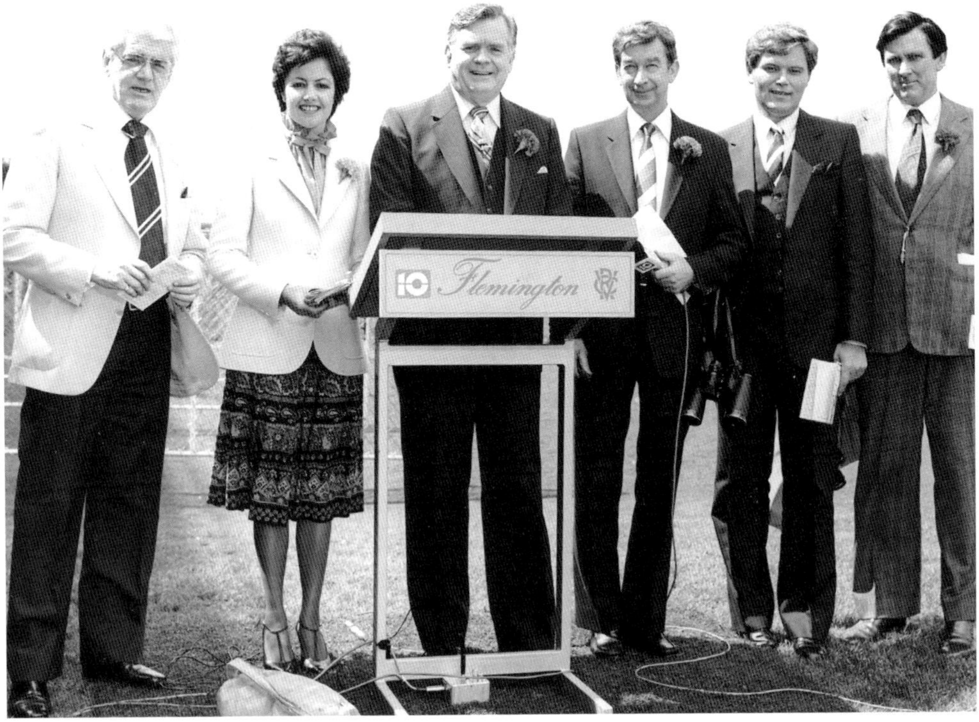

Channel 10's Melbourne Cup Racing Panel in the 1980s. From left: Peter Lovitt, Vivienne Smith, Philip Gibbs, Ron Taylor, Clem Dimsey, Graeme Kelly.

When this man talks racing, Melbourne listens.

Ron Taylor, who has been the Racing Editor of Truth for 20 years, has a reputation as one of the most respected racing journalists in Australia.

He is a fearless commentator; hard hitting when the occasion demands, but always fair. He barracks for the punter and keeps the stewards on their toes.

When it comes to racing Ron Taylor can discuss it on all levels, and with genuine authority. When he talks to David Grant, Harry Beitzel and Bill Jacobs on the 3AW Saturday Morning Sports Show, 10.00 am to noon, he is as informative as he is knowledgeable. Tune into Ron and the winning team on 3AW this Saturday.

1278 LIFE OF THE CITY
3AW

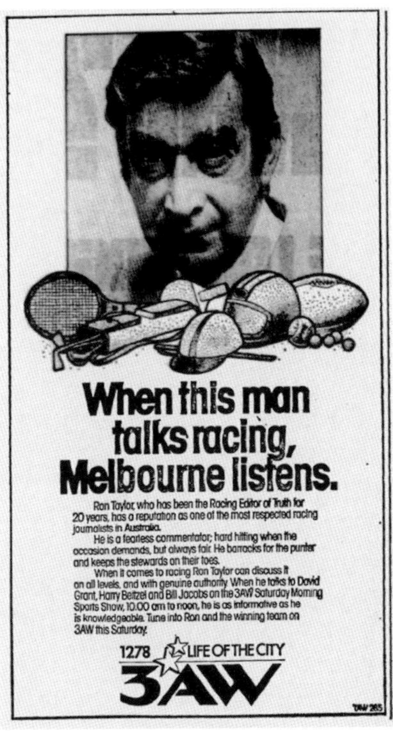

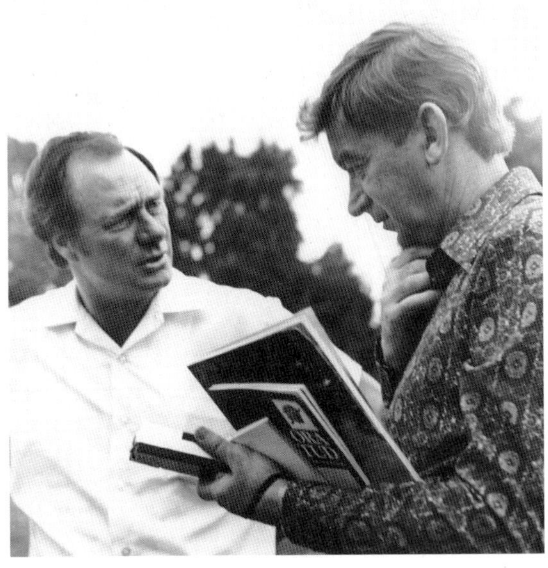

Ron chats with NZ trainer Colin Jillings at Karaka.

Left: 3AW advertising Ron's radio programme.

Ron and Jack Klugman when Jack was a guest columnist for *Truth Racing* on a visit to Australia.

Ron's favourite self taken photo of the start of a race at Auteuil Hippodrome racecourse just outside Paris. The starter oblivious of how he looks from behind.

Ron aged 63 (Essendon) and Philip Opas, 74 (Geelong) contest a mark during a kick-to kick session at Yarra Park in 1991.

Harry White wins the 1987 W.S.Cox plate on Rubiton. Background left is Mike Willisee and right Moonie Valley Secretary Ian McEwen.

Jack Elliott strikes a chord with Ron's wife Lola as he shares a joke with Ron and Jack Ayling.

Michael Pitt (fawn suit, centre) doing his settling at the Victoria Club.

Ron and Peter Moody August 2011.

Two great champions Roy Higgins and George Moore.

Proud Miss as a yearling... the one that got away!

Paper Girl being broken in as a yearling by Brian Hall.

Champion American racehorse Secretariat at stud in America. Insert: Statue of Secretariat at Belmont Park.

David Hains with his champion Kingston Town.

"SPERO GIOLMAN"
GOLDEN GATE FIELDS, CALIF. 5/20/77 MERLIN VOLZKE, UP
MAIN EVENTER, (2nd) 6 FUR-1:10:4 TONY LEP, (3rd)
ATKINS, GUERIN & PAPIANO, OWNER C. A. COMISKEY, TRAINER
"THE PHAR LAP"

Ron and Lola making a presentation at Golden Gate Fields in the USA, 1977. Lola is about to present the bauquet.

Colin Hayes at trackwork with Brent Thompson.

The 'two ronnies' Ron with Ron Hutchinson both aged 90.

Trailblazer Therese Payne.

Dormello Stud, Italy. Mares and foals in idyllic surroundings on the edge of Lake Maggiore.

Dulcify winning the VRC Derby in 1978. Colin Hayes was the trainer, ridden by Brett Thomson.

The safer re-modelled steeplechase fence after the industry review.

Bart Cummings foreman Leon Corstens with VRC vet Dr John Burke.

Group of *Truth Racing* Tour members in Japan. Well known trainer Kel Chapman is on the right.

Ron interviewing Jim Cassidy after winning the Melbourne Cup on Kiwi in 1983.

Truth boys get together at the Boathouse Maribyrnong just before Ron's 90th birthday. L–R: Tony de Bolfo, Glenn Huxley, Gary Watt, Danny Power, Daryl Timms, Geoff Poulter, Tony Kneebone, Peter Taylor, Ron Taylor.

of his ride when he was beaten on the 11/4 on favourite Sobar in the Victoria Derby of 1972.

Sobar, who had won the Caulfield Guineas and the Caulfield Cup, was being hailed as the best horse in the country and was labelled a good thing in the Derby. But Harry got caught out on a limb and he travelled three and four horses wide from the barrier until he hit the front at the top of the straight.

In the end the extra ground he had covered, plus the fact Sobar had pulled and reefed for most of the trip, told on him. He was beaten by Dayana who had stormed home to win by a neck. Harry took the blame, but what he didn't know, and neither did anyone else in the immediate aftermath, was that the colt had sprung a tendon during the race.

The injury didn't become apparent until after the horse had cooled down, and the full significance of it wasn't realised until the Monday morning when a decision had to be made whether he could run in the Melbourne Cup the following day.

Sobar's trainer Ken Hilton and the owner Keith Southwick called in the respected veterinary surgeon Greg Morrison to give his opinion. Sobar was trotted and cantered on the grass at Caulfield in front of Mr. Morrison who then examined the leg. He told the connections that as there was a swelling in the near fore fetlock joint, the horse should not run in the Cup.

The die was cast. Sobar was out, and so were the many thousands of dollars Mr. Southwick would have won had Sobar been successful. He had coupled the horse heavily in doubles to win both the Caulfield and Melbourne Cups and the odds were heavily in his favour for a collect. But it was not to be. Sobar did recover to race again but he was never the same horse.

Harry however did go on to great success. He won four Melbourne Cups, a record he shares with Bobbie Lewis. Harry won on Think Big in 1974 and 1975, and on Arwon 1978 and Hyperno 1979. We have remained friends all through the years although we don't often see each other these days with Harry battling multiple sclerosis in Gisborne and me growing old in Carlton. But that's life.

The jockey ranks have changed dramatically since I reported my first race meeting back in 1948 due mainly to an influx of female riders. Now about 30 per cent of the riding force are women and the rate is growing. When I started, women were not allowed to ride in professional races against men.

At first, I didn't think the girls would last. I didn't think they had the skills, strength and stamina of the men. They have since proved me wrong.

The two trail blazers were Pam O'Neill in Queensland, and Linda Jones from New Zealand. Linda, aged 27, but still an apprentice under NZ rules, was the first female jockey to ride against men in Australia. Linda rode Northfleet, trained by her husband Alan, at Rosehill in March 1979. She only ran third that day but went on to ride 48 winners in a limited career.

Pam O'Neill, was 34 when she had her first professional ride just a few weeks after Linda. But Pam's debut was more auspicious. She rode three winners at Southport on the Gold Coast. The success of these two pioneering young women led to many young girls wanting to become jockeys and it's a situation that has gained momentum as the years have moved on.

The first young girl I encountered was Therese Payne, the older sister of Michelle who won the 2015 Melbourne Cup on Prince Of Penzance. Therese was only 14 when she received her licence and conditions at that time were very primitive for lady riders. Most tracks didn't have a separate room for female jockeys and they had to change in the Ladies' Toilet.

I must admit Therese surprised me with her skills and how well horses ran for her. She rode 450 winners before giving up riding to start training and, in that time, many other young girls followed her footsteps.

I think I really came around to accept that the females could match it with the boys when Bart Cummings put Michelle Payne on the 40/1 chance Alllez Wonder in the Group 1 Toorak Handicap in 2009.

Michelle rode a copybook race settling midfield, one off the fence, moving forward before the home turn, finding a gap on straightening, then pushing through to win convincingly. Bart was sufficiently impressed to put her on again in the Melbourne Cup, but Allez Wonder couldn't stay the trip and finished 16th.

I thought at the time that if it was good enough for the best trainer of stayers in Australia to put a female jockey on in the Melbourne Cup, then who was I to doubt his wisdom? Bart had given the girls the green light and that was good enough for me.

I was reminded of that 2009 Toorak Handicap when in 2015, the leading trainer at the time, Darren Weir, engaged Michelle to ride Prince of Penzance in the Melbourne Cup. I wondered if history might repeat itself.

Prince of Penzance was 100/1, which in my opinion was over the odds, but no female jockey had ever won the Melbourne Cup so the bookies weren't taking much of a risk. My main bet in the Cup that year was the German horse Our Ivanhowe, who had run third in the Caulfield Cup, but I did have a 'saver' on Prince of Penzance. Michelle gave him a peach of a ride to win comfortably from Max Dynamite and Criterion. Our Ivanhowe failed to stay, finishing tenth.

Michelle certainly struck a blow for the ladies and her success has encouraged more young girls to become jockeys. In fact, the apprentice jockey school gets so many applications from young girls they have to turn several away.

And if any further proof was needed that the girls have reached equality, you only have to look at the number of Group One winners they have ridden.

At the time of writing, Michelle heads the list so far with five, followed by Claire Lindop (four), Kathy O'Hara (two), Jamie Kah (two) and Linda Meech (two). Four other girls have ridden one each: Nikita Beriman, Katelyn Mallyon, Lauren Stojakovic and Rachael King. Not a bad effort when you consider some of the boys they ride against haven't ridden any.

31

Bart Had A Heart

I met most of the top trainers in Australia during my career, well, a lot of them anyway, and the three I knew best were Bart Cummings, Tommy Smith and Colin Hayes. That was only natural I suppose because they were the ones who were always winning.

I won't go into details about their careers because everyone knows their history: like how Bart won a record 12 Melbourne Cups, Tommy won 35 consecutive Sydney trainers' premierships and Colin 28 Adelaide premierships and 13 in Melbourne. All three have been promoted to Legend status in the Australian Racing Hall of Fame.

So I'll confine myself to writing a little about them from the personal angle, how they impacted on me as men, not just as horse trainers. There were so many shades to Bart he was like a Chameleon, changing his mood to suit the occasion. He could be funny, serious, thrifty, generous, laconic, loquacious, tough, gentle, good hearted—you would need a thesaurus to try to find enough words to describe him.

He didn't mind taking the mickey out of you if he was in the mood for a bit of fun. Trackwork time can get a bit boring between gallops and Bart was always on the look-out for a circuit breaker. I copped it one morning when I was doing radio interviews for 3AW. My job was to ask Bart how Light Fingers (for example) had worked that morning and take the tape back to the radio station for broadcast.

The interview would go like this: 'Good morning Bart, how did Light Fingers work this morning?'

'Well, Des (referring to Des Spain the well-known clocker at Flemington) she's in fine fettle.'

'Stop!' I would say. 'Fair go Bart. Let's start again.'

'Well Des,' he would repeat causing me to stop the tape and again.

'Fair crack of the whip Bart,' I would say, 'let's be serious. I'm recording.'

Then he would grin and say: 'Sorry, Ron, you can start again now.'

That was Bart, he had a quirky sense of humour, like those one-liners he was famous for. The most often quoted is the one about the flies. I'll repeat it in case someone might have missed it. One morning the Health Inspector visited Bart's stables and said: 'You've got too many flies here.' Bart fired back: 'Well, how many should I have?'

Another one I liked was at the time Bart's jockey Darren Beadman got religion and decided to retire. When Bart was informed that God had told Darren to hang up his saddle he answered: 'I think he should get a second opinion.'

I discovered there was a human side to Bart when I was in Tokyo for the Japan Cup in 1992. I had gone along to the offices of the Japan Racing Association to present my Press credentials and to pick up the necessary tickets. Bart was standing at the counter waiting for assistance. We exchanged greetings and Bart said: 'Why haven't you got one of these?' pointing to the bomber jacket he was wearing.

It was a neat looking fawn coloured nylon garment, hip

length with a zipper up the front and a very neat little logo over the heart with the inscription 'Japan Cup 92'. I told Bart I wasn't entitled to one, they were only for the connections of horses running in the Japan Cup. 'Be blowed to that,' replied to Bart. 'Come with me.'

Bart led me out of the office, down a corridor to a room that contained row after row of these Japan Cup bomber jackets. 'What size are you?' Bart asks. 'Small, medium? Here's a medium, try this on,' he says pulling a jacket off the rack. 'No,' I say, 'I can't take it.'

'Yes you can, it's yours,' Bart says.

Who am I to argue with this great man? So I put it on and go back to the office to pick up my tickets. Nobody queries me so I cop the jacket and I've still got it today. It's quite a dressy garment, not at all horsey looking, so I've made a lot of use of it.

That's the kind of man Bart was. He could be sending you up one minute then being thoughtful and generous the next. Other people would have different ideas about him, but to me as a working reporter, he was always approachable and helpful when I was looking for news. In my vernacular he was a 'good bloke'.

Bart Cummings.

32

Tommy's Melbourne Cup Woes

Tommy Smith was different, always open-hearted, ready to please, easy to read. Tommy loved life, he loved champagne, particularly when laced with orange juice. He loved parties, he loved dining out with friends. Although I didn't see as much of Tommy as I did of Bart I can still claim him as a friend.

Tommy never let me down when I was looking for a story. If he didn't have one, he would make one up. But he wasn't that way just with me, he was the same with all reporters.

As a horse trainer Tommy's record was impeccable. He ruled the roost in Sydney for more than 30 years. In that time his horses won 35 AJC Derbies. He won 33 consecutive Sydney training premierships, seven W.S Cox Plates, six Golden Slippers, and two Melbourne Cups. They didn't come any better than that.

I remember calling him one afternoon when looking for a story and found him in a talkative mood. He started to tell me what a great horse Redcraze was and then reminisced about his other Melbourne Cup runners. 'You know, Ron,' he said, 'I should have trained about eight Melbourne Cup winners.

'If you go back through my horses, Redcraze, Gunsynd, Tulloch—jeez, there were some morals beaten. That Redcraze, it was pitiful. I remember he should have won two Melbourne Cups for me, the day he ran second, and the next year when he ran fourth (actually it was eighth). He never had any luck in the Melbourne Cup each time he ran.

'He had 10 stone something (10st.3lb) the day the mare got up and beat him (Evening Peal, 1956). It was like Kingston Town. He finished right under the Judges Box, and his jockey Arthur Ward had that much lead under the saddle it started to slip back, and he couldn't kick. And when he would go to kick him his little legs stuck out and he couldn't kick back, and when he should have got out Arthur knocked up. He got tired as buggery and couldn't ride the horse out.

'The next year, I've never seen anything like it. He never stopped getting knocked over, poor old bugger, he was stuck out in no man's land, and ran fourth or fifth (eighth).'

You had to take a lot of what Tommy said with a grain of salt. He did get carried away at times. He had great respect for Arthur Ward as a jockey and appointed him as his stable rider when George Moore was suspended. Even when Moore came back after two years and resumed his No.1 role Tommy kept Arthur on Redcraze because he had such a good record on him.

Referring to Kingston Town's Melbourne Cup Tommy said: 'He wasn't bred to run two miles, but he could run two miles. If he was sound, and if he could have run on the Saturday (LKS Mackinnon Stakes day), I'd have run him on the Saturday, but I was frightened that if he ran—Percy Sykes, the vet, said to me: "I wouldn't run him, Tommy, he might pull up lame," and I thought, well, if he is going to pull up lame he might as well pull up lame in the Melbourne Cup.

'He should have run on the Saturday, it would have topped him off, he was just a little bit underdone. I like horses to race and be fit, particularly horses that haven't raced much. I like hard, fit buggers. He fought all the way (in the Cup). He had a hellava hard job. Malcolm (Johnston) took him to the front, he didn't go on the fence and he stayed out in the middle of the track. He shot well clear, he could have gone over to the fence, but he stayed out in the centre.'

It's history now that Gurner's Lane, under Mick Dittman's desperate riding, got through on the rails and beat Kington Town by a neck. It was a deceptive finish because the horses were wide apart, and Tommy, who was watching from the Trainers' Reserve in the Members Stand, about 200 metres short of the winning post, thought Kingston Town had won. He was not alone, and dozens of friends and well-wishers rushed to congratulate him.

But they were premature. Grins turned to tears when it was realised that the angle had deceived them and Gurner's Lane, not Kingston Town, had won the prize. Tommy took it philosophically, he'd had disappointments before. As they say in the classics: 'That's racing.'

Jockey Mick Dittman with Tommy Smith and Kingstown Town. Note how Tommy was always impeccably dressed, even at trackwork.

33

The Hayes Dynasty

Colin Hayes was the third member of this training triumvirate with Cummings and Smith, a treble that dominated so many of the big races from the 1960s through to the '90s. Colin had the skills of Bart and Tommy, he just employed them in different ways. Again, I had a very good relationship with Colin, although it generally was on a working basis.

Colin was based in Adelaide where he operated out of his training and breeding facility at Lindsay Park in the Barossa Valley. So I didn't see a lot of him except at carnival time in the spring and autumn when he came to Melbourne. But there was one occasion when the personal side of our friendship became apparent.

It was approaching Christmas and as I was about to leave Flemington after trackwork, Colin pulled up in his car alongside mine. 'Hang on a minute, Ron,' he said, 'I've got something for you.' He went to the boot of his car and took out a package. 'Happy Xmas,' he said and handed me a presentation pack of Yalumba wines. I really appreciated the gesture because, if I was writing stories about him, I was only doing my job, the same as I would be doing regarding any other trainer.

For all I know Colin gave the same package to all the racing writers but, whether he did or not, I took it as a personal gesture. That's the sort of man he was. There was something Edwardian about him, very proper, very mannerly. It showed in his dress too. He was always impeccably attired, English style, houndstooth jackets, Trilby hats.

As a trainer he was an innovator. He embraced the idea that horses did better in a country atmosphere compared to the circuitous training on city tracks. To prove his point he purchased, with the help of a small syndicate, Lindsay Park, a 400-acre property at Angaston, roughly 80km from Adelaide in 1965.

It took him five years or so to transform the property into the establishment he had envisaged and, when complete, it was the most modern training complex in Australia.

Not long after Colin had got it all set up I asked if I could come across and write a story about it for *Truth*'s racing magazine *Bred To Win*. He said he would be happy to show me around, so, a few days later, I turned up with photographer Allan 'Spider' Funnel and we spent a whole day there.

My outstanding memory of that day was Colin telling me that he had designed the training track to follow the contours of Warren Hill, the famous training ground at Newmarket in England where the ground rises 40 metres in the last two furlongs.

Colin didn't go quite that far, containing his rise to 25 metres in the last three furlongs. He worked on the principle that the English trainers had success because they worked their horses uphill 'into the collar'. 'It's a method that has stood the test of time,' he explained.

The move from Adelaide to Angaston proved to be the catalyst for Hayes' outstanding success as a trainer. There were many doubters and naysayers however who predicted the move was doomed to failure.

Several clients took their horses away, and in his first season at Lindsay Park his team was reduced by more than half. Yet he still trained 102 winners to give him his best season for seven years.

Once Colin had proved his point, his career took off. His success attracted attention overseas and leading English owner Robert Sangster joined his stable as did Sheik Hamdan bin Rashid Al Maktoum. Both these men made huge contributions to Colin's success and he repaid both by winning Melbourne Cups for them… Beldale Ball for Robert and At Talaq for Sheik Hamdan.

Sadly, Colin passed away in 1999 at the age of 75. He had been retired for nine years but the Hayes name still carried on with son Peter looking after the Adelaide and Melbourne operations, and David doing his own thing in Hong Kong. I didn't see much of David because he was overseas, but I did get on well with Peter when he took over.

It took a while to get to know him though. Peter had a different nature to Colin and David. He didn't say a lot and, for starters, I almost had to drag the news out of him. But as the days went on and he became accustomed to me asking questions he did relax and if he could help me, he would.

Peter tragically died in a plane crash in 2001 when he was only 52 and David has returned to Hong Kong after setting up a showplace training establishment at Euroa. I retired in 1993 and don't have any involvement with the family any more other than to say 'Hi' to David at the races and sometimes have a brief chat.

But the legacy Colin Hayes left behind is still a major force in Australian racing. More and more trainers are following his example and setting up country properties or going to country racecourses to train. David's son Ben was running Euroa alongside David's nephew Tom Dabering, until Tom decided to branch out on his own. Just as is the case with Bart Cummings and Tommy Smith, Colin Hayes' work is being carried on by his family.

34

Tony Lopes Was 'Hands On'

Now that I have told you about the three best trainers during my time, I want to tell you about some who didn't get the top awards, or win all the biggest races, but men who turned out winners almost every Saturday. They were the backbone of the industry.

But first, I must add the name Lee Freedman to those I have mentioned as Australia's top trainers. I feel comfortable to talk about Lee in the same context as Tommy, Bart and Colin, because of his outstanding contribution to Australian racing.

Lee came from Sydney to set up stables in Melbourne in 1984 when he wasn't quite 30, and when he arrived at Flemington he came like a breath of fresh air. He was young, exuberant, intelligent, and he raised the tone of training there to a new level.

I soon found out Lee was all about business and winning. He didn't have time for idle chatter with me at those early morning track sessions, but when I asked a direct question I got a direct answer.

Lee's business-like approach attracted a more high-profile list of clients who were able to provide him with a better class of horse. I watched as his team went from strength to strength, highlighted by the 1989 Melbourne Cup when he quinella-ed the race with Tawriffic and Super Impose.

From then on Lee had a meteoric rise, but it was destined

not to last. In the seven years following his Melbourne Cup success with Tawriffic he won two more Melbourne Cups with Subzero and Doriemus. In the same period he won four successive Golden Slippers, as well as two AJC Derbies and two Victoria Derbies.

This was the early 1990s when Lee had such stable stars as Schillaci, Mahogany, and Mannerism and those brilliant two-year-olds Bint Marscay, Danzero, Flying Spur and Merlene.

Lee's stables became known as the FBI—Freedman Brothers Incorporated, comprising Lee, Richard, Anthony and Michael. They could do no wrong. Super Impose won two Doncasters and two Epsoms and a W.S. Cox Plate.

On the crest of this wave Lee won the Victorian trainers' premiership for the first time in 1997, ending 19 years of successive wins by the Hayes family: Colin, David and Peter. Then in 2003 he was admitted to the Australian Racing Hall of Fame.

That's why I considered Lee worthy to be spoken of in the same breath as Smith, Cummings and Hayes. But it wasn't to last.

Looking for greener pastures Lee transferred his stables from Flemington to Caulfield and bought country properties at Balnarring and Rye to diversify his training methods.

During this period Lee had some of his greatest success. In 2004 he took over the training the 2003 Melbourne Cup winner Makybe Diva from David Hall and won the 2004 Cup with her. He did it again in 2005 to give Makybe Diva an unprecedented three successive Melbourne Cup wins.

Also at this time Lee was preparing the crack sprinter Miss Andretti, whom he took to England and won the King's Stand Stakes. No further proof was need that he had established himself as one of Australia's greatest trainers.

But the pressure of training took its toll leading to Lee's marriage break-up and a bout of depression. In 2011 he decided to retire from training and handed over the reins to his brother Anthony.

For a while he took a new direction and became Racing Director for his friend and long-time client Lloyd Williams and was in charge of running his property Macedon Lodge.

But the lure of the racetrack proved too great and in 2014 Lee was back training in partnership with Anthony. By this time I had long since retired from *Truth* and had lost close contact with Lee. But naturally, I followed his career from the sidelines, wanting him to succeed.

Lee was always looking ahead, looking for a new challenge, so I wasn't surprised in 2017 when he applied for a trainers' licence in Singapore, and even less surprised when it was granted. In his first full season there he was the leading trainer. Lee has since returned to Australia and is setting up stables on the Gold Coast.

At one time, after he had trained his fifth Melbourne Cup winner in 2005, I thought Lee might do the impossible and train more Melbourne Cup winners than Bart Cummings. At that time Bart had won the Cup 11 times and increased that number to 12 when Viewed was successful in 2008.

It would need a miracle for that to happen now. Lee is 64 and needs eight Cup winners to break Bart's record. But don't be surprised if Lee has a crack at it and at least adds to his tally. We'll see.

Now let me get back to telling you about some of the other trainers I knew who have made their mark on racing without necessarily reaching the top of the tree.

One I had the most contact with was Tony Lopes, who I mentioned earlier as the trainer of the ill-starred Paper Girl. Tony is best known as the trainer of the champion mare Chicquita, who had some heroic tussles with another champion, Comic Court.

I didn't see Chicquita race, as I was 'on the desk' at Radio Australia during her mighty three-year-old career, but I knew all about her. The stories of her clashes with Comic Court are legendary. They met 12 times and Comic Court beat her home on 10 occasions, so I guess you would have to say he was superior. But seven times they ran the quinella, including the most famous one in the 1950 Melbourne Cup, which Comic Court won.

Tony didn't speak to me a lot about Chiquita other than to reminisce one morning about her winning her first race at Caulfield, when the betting plunge was so big he had to bring the money home in a suitcase.

Tony was a hands-on, old-time trainer who didn't rely on vets all that much. He used to say his vet was Dr. Green (meaning green as in grass). When he took over the training of Gay Icarus following a disagreement between the owners, he found the horse had a problem with one of its legs which he couldn't fathom.

Gay Icarus was the leading three-year-old in the autumn of 1970, winning the Australian Cup, the Australasian Champion Stakes, and the AJC Queen Elizabeth Stakes. In the spring he went on to take the Caulfield Cup. But when Tony got him two years later, he was past his best.

Nevertheless, Tony believed that if he could cure the leg problem he could get another win out of him. So he walked across the road from his Chicquita Lodge stables in Smithfield Road to the Flemington Abattoirs, and bought the leg of a recently slaughtered thoroughbred.

He took it back to his stables, opened it up, and traced the ligaments and tendons all the way down the canon bone to the fetlock, until he was thoroughly familiar with every working part. When he was satisfied he had the answer, he prepared Gay Icarus for the spring of 1973 and won the Craiglee Stakes at Flemington with him.

Tony did such a marvellous job of getting Gay Icarus back to form that he started favourite in the Caulfield Cup the following year. Ridden by Ron Hall Jnr. he ran a game and courageous fourth to Leilani. It was his last race.

Among the other good horses Tony trained were Bowl King, Pablo Star, Timetheus, St. Joel, Stop The Show, Caboul and Comicquita, the son of a mating between those two great rivals Comic Court and Chicquita.

I raced several horses with Tony over the years, in partnerships with others, and we had some success. The lesson I learned from that experience is that luck plays such an important role in racing. Of course you knew that anyway. But it hits home harder when it concerns yourself, as it did one day at Ballarat when I thought our horse was a 'good thing'.

The horse was Fort Lauderdale whom Tony had leased from Glenn Stott, a well-known breeder who had a small stud out Oaklands Junction way. Fort Lauderdale was a chunky little fellow, a real sprinting type, and he showed Tony ability right from the get-go. So Tony takes him to Ballarat for his first start, a maiden over five furlongs.

We engage Jimmy Johnson to ride him and get 9/2 for our money. He bolts in by three lengths with Jimmy sitting against him. So we think it is just a piece of cake when he returns to Ballarat for his next start in an Improvers' Handicap. As expected, he jumps to the front and settles beautifully in the lead.

Suddenly, after about 100 yards, he dips, goes down on his nose and it's all over. He struggles to his feet but his leg is broken. He had to be put down on the spot. What caused him to stumble and fall I don't know. It didn't matter anyway—the poor horse was gone. Jimmy was OK thank goodness.

I did have better luck ten years later when Ross du Bourg, a colleague at *Truth*, offered me a quarter share in the lease of a filly he had bought with his mother Jessica. Ross was an expert on pedigrees and he was looking to breed from this filly after she retired.

Ross loved music, particularly operas. So I'm sure it was his knowledge of musical terms that caused him to name the filly Cabaletta. I like music myself, but it wasn't until I consulted the Internet that I discovered why Ross had made this choice. I found that the word 'cabaletta' was probably a derivative of the Italian word 'cavallo', meaning horse.

In musical terms the 'cabaletta' is the fast portion of a two-part aria and has been likened to the pulsating rhythm of a galloping horse. This would have appealed to Ross as he was quite fastidious about everything he did.

I remember when he joined me as co-Editor on the magazine *Bred To Win* he insisted that every time we referred to an imported horse it must carry an asterisk* next to it name, denoting that it came from overseas.

I thought if we used the asterisk, or the letters in brackets (imp), the first time we mentioned the horse's name that would have been sufficient. But not to Ross. He believed the asterisk should be treated as part of the horse's name and always used in conjunction with it.

So Cabaletta went to Tony Lopes to be trained and she turned out quite useful. She was a staying bred filly by the English two-miler Proper Pride, so we didn't expect much from her early. However she was able to win a two-year-old race over 1400 metres at Seymour towards the end of the 1973 season, so we had hopes she might be an Oaks filly.

It was not to be, but she did win her second race 20 months later when Brian Andrews rode her to victory over 2600 metres at Moonee Valley. Not long after this Ross decided it was time to put her to stud, so off she went to the breeding barn. She turned out a very good broodmare.

Cabaletta had ten foals and six of them won races. There were no stars, but Heart of Egypt, Jewel of Egypt and Dynamic Dancer all won city races. I didn't have any involvement with these horses but kept up my friendship with Ross until he passed away a few years ago.

Ross was a lovely fellow, a thorough gentleman and a pleasure to know. His knowledge of pedigrees was amazing and he became an international authority. After his death his friends and executors, Brian and Tim Kelly, presented me with a framed portrait of Cabaletta which Ross had commissioned when she was in her prime. It's a beautiful painting and has pride of place in my study.

Two trainers who were so very helpful to me in those early days when I was attending trackwork at Flemington were John Sadler and John Meagher.

John Sadler hadn't long come down from Colac, and had secured two very good horses, Jolly Old Mac and Lady Jakeo. I was still working for *Truth* and through my early morning chats with John was able to keep our readers up to date with the progress of these two horses. Jolly Old Mac won the Australian Guineas and Lady Jacko took out the Blue Diamond Stakes.

I soon learned that John was not only a good judge of his own horses' ability but those of rival trainers as well. We would often swap opinions on how, maybe, one of Bart's, or Colin's, was going and these chats were a big help when it came to doing my tips for Saturday's races.

I got to know John Meagher when he was training Star of the Realm and soon found out what a meticulous trainer he was. John always rode a pony and directed his team from horseback. The pony gave him extra mobility and he was johnny-on-the-spot when his horses returned after a gallop to see how they pulled up.

Star of The Realm won the Victoria Derby in 1991 to give John another big Group one success following his Melbourne Cup win with What a Nuisance in 1985. John left Australia towards the end of 1990 and trained in Singapore for 11 years before returning to Australia where he has set up a partnership with his son Chris. He was inducted into the Australian Racing Hall of Fame in 2019.

I can only speak from the heart about trainers with whom I had a personal relationship, like those I have mentioned, but I had a good relationship with all the trainers. They were all obliging, well, barring one or two.

However I would not be telling you the true story of my career if I didn't mention the friendships I also forged with the stable foremen of the top trainers. They were always there to help me identify a certain horse or fill me in with the work it might be doing, or to answer my questions if they could.

There was Gary Fennessy, foreman for Colin Hayes; the late Ron McDonell, foreman for Bart Cummings, and his successors Leon Corstens and Nigel Blackiston. It makes my day now when I go to the races and get a nod, or a smile, or a handshake from Gary, or Leon or Nigel. Then I know those golden days when Colin and Bart were in their prime are not forgotten.

And I couldn't leave this period of my life if I didn't mention the help I received from Bart's trackrider, Joe Agresta. Joe was such an integral part of Bart's team. He rode so many of Bart's champions in their gallops, horses such as Let's Elope, Kingston Rule, Saintly, Shaftesbury Avenue, So You Think, Stylish Century—the list is endless.

Joe's first responsibility was always to Bart, but if he could share some knowledge without giving too much away, he was always happy to chat. Joe has since written a book called

Trackrider and it's a wonderful insight into his relationship with Bart and the part he played in helping him achieve so much Melbourne Cup success. I still see Joe at the races and we enjoy reminiscing about those early mornings at Flemington where history was being forged.

35

In Italy

Let's now get away from the racing scene and look at life in retirement—if there ever has been such a thing for me. Even though it is now 27 years since I left *Truth*, I have never really retired. Once racing is in your blood it is there forever. Until the coronavirus came along in 2020 I hardly missed a race meeting, the lure of the track was too strong.

And, I think, once a journalist you are always a journalist. I have never lost the desire to write and that's the reason I am sitting down now and recounting some of the adventures I have experienced, and some of the associations I have made. If I am a good journalist these stories will entertain you—well, you will be the judge of that.

The first thing I wanted to do after leaving *Truth* was to take a break. Work had become monotonous. Doing the same thing day after day, following the same routine, had lost its glamour. I had never been out of a job from the time I turned 17 until I reached 65. It was time for a change.

Ever since I was a kid I had wanted to go to Italy to see the place where my grandfather, Peter Varena, was born. At school I used to pull out the atlas and open it up at northern Italy and try to pick out the town of Grosio where he was born.

Grosio was only a dot on the map, and hard to find, but

when I did locate it I would sit there dreaming about what it would be like to visit.

That was, until I was rudely shaken out of my reverie by a piece of chalk, flicked from the teacher's ruler, striking me on the head. He rarely missed did Mr. King, but it did have the desired effect of waking me up and making me pay attention. Nevertheless I still dreamed that one day I would visit Italy and see Grosio for myself.

I did eventually make that dream a reality when Lola and I took a holiday in 1984. The main purpose was to make that long awaited visit to the relatives, but there were other sights to see along the way.

I thought the best way to do it was to hire a car in Paris and drive to Grosio, stopping off at some of the beautiful places along the way. It was a long trip, took us seven days, but well worth it. We had stops at Geneva, Stressa, Montreaux and Lake Como before completing the trip, which I reckon would have exceeded 1200km.

So we arrive at our hotel in Grosio just before lunch time and book in. The proprietor, Jim Pini, is expecting us and turns us over to his Manager who says: 'After you have settled down I will take you to see your relatives.' But Lola says: 'Blow to that, let's go and find them for ourselves.'

So we walk into the main street looking for the Town Hall. It wasn't hard to find so in we go and I soon find a large room where clerks are busily working at their desks. I front up to the counter and a man of about my age inquires if there is anything he can do for us.

I reply, in the best Italian I can muster, that I am the grandson of Pietro Varenna, a former inhabitant of Grosio, and that I am looking for some information on his family.

'Si, si, capito,' he replies, and moves away to a high wall that is stacked with leather-bound volumes. He climbs a ladder to the top shelf where he extracts one of the volumes and brings it to the counter.

He opens it up and starts running his finger down one of the pages: 'Varenna,' he says, 'Pietro?' I say 'si' and he continues his search down the page. 'Ah!' he says, 'do you mean Pietro, the son of Pietro Varenna and Paolina Pini?' I tell him I do, so he keeps going down the page, 'Ah,' he says again, 'here is Pietro, and his brother and sisters. Anna, Maria, Antonia, Giuseppe and Lucia... Lucia!' he exclaims loudly, 'Lucia is my mother. We are cousins.'

With that he jumps the counter, puts his arm arms around me and keeps repeating, 'cugino, cugino' (cousin). Then he is on the telephone, comes back and says: 'You must come with me and have lunch with my sister.'

'No, no,' I reply politely, 'we couldn't possibly.' Then I feel a sharp pain in my ankle where Lola has kicked me. 'Well, if you really think so, yes we will come,' I hastily add.

By the time we reach his sister Domenica's house there is already a small gathering. Relatives have come from nowhere. It's a convivial group and arrangements are made for all the relations to get together at Jim Pini's Sarsella Hotel for a celebration dinner that evening.

There must have been about 20 rolled up and there was lots of talk and lots of wine. There wasn't much English spoken, but because we were all family, it didn't matter. We just kept smiling and drinking.

Next day, my mother's cousin, Guiseppe, took Lola and I on a tour of the town. It was a pleasant little village with a population of around 4,500 and, I was told, very popular with tourists and bicycle riders. We were very comfortable at Jim Pini's

Hotel but after a couple of days it was time to move on.

I won't bore you with stories of the rest of the trip other than to say if you ever get the chance to spend time in Sorrento, don't miss it.

Finally, in 1993 I decided to call it quits at *Truth*. I nominated the last day of the racing season for my final appearance and, when the Sunset Handicap was run that day at Moonee Valley, I bowed out.

That's when I started to plan my retirement. What I had seen of cities like Rome, Florence and Venice on *Truth*'s Racing Tours had only whetted my appetite to see more of Italy. Retirement offered that opportunity.

I figured the best way to do it was to go to Italy and live there for a year. I had some superannuation coming to me for all the years I worked at *Truth*, so I spent it on buying a townhouse in Carlton, which I rented out. I reckoned the rent from Carlton would about equal the rent of a villa in countryside Italy. It turned out about the same, near enough, so the main expense was taken care of.

Then, if I was going to stay for a year, I would need a car. If I bought it in Italy I could avoid paying tax, unless I wanted to bring it back to Australia with me. But I reckoned I could get rid of it over there. So, working though the Italian Consulate in Melbourne and the Fiat Company in Turin in Italy, I was able to buy a brand new Fiat Uno, duty free, for around $10,000.

But, of course, I had to go to Italy and pay the money before I could take delivery. No problem, the money was wired to a bank in Turin for me to pick up. Then all I had to do was go to the Fiat factory and collect the car. Which proved easier said than done, however.

My wife and I get to Turin and turn up at the factory on

the appointed day. We are greeted by a salesman who says: 'Scusa, I'm sorry, the car is ready but the registration papers have not turned up. You will have to wait a week.'

I hadn't counted on spending a week in Turin and expressed my displeasure to the man. But he just shrugged and said something like: 'This is Italy, everything takes time. Why do you want to come here anyway? There is depression, unemployment, unstable Government. It's a crazy country.'

He wasn't a very happy sort of soul and wanted to know what I would do with the car when I left Italy. I told him I would sell it. 'How will you do that? You don't know the language, there is a lot of paperwork, you would not understand.'

I said something like 'don't worry, I'll manage,' even though I didn't have a clue. I thought, I'll deal with that when the time comes. I didn't want to take the car home because I didn't need it there.

Anyway, to take the car home would have negated the whole idea of buying it in the first place. The thinking behind that idea was that it would be much cheaper to buy the car than to rent one for a year.

36

House Hunting In Tuscany

So it looks like we are stuck in Turin for a week, but Lola had another idea. 'Why don't we hire a car and go and look at your mate's villa in Greve in Tuscany?' she said.

Lola was referring to a former colleague who had tossed in his job in Sydney to go and live in Italy, teach a bit of English and make ends meet by dabbling in real estate. I had written to him asking if he could recommend a small villa in Tuscany that would suit my budget. He replied he had some friends in Greve who would be willing to rent their house (it was more like a chateau) as they could do with a holiday themselves.

The price was more than I wanted to pay, but I wrote back and said we would be happy to look at it, but our decision would depend on whether we liked it or not. So I go to the car rental in Turin and hire out a Hyundi Pony for a week.

On the way to Greve we pass by the city of Lucca, and I decide this would be a good place to break the journey.

We book into a hotel and the following morning take a stroll around the city, happening to pass a real estate shop. So we look in the window to see what's for rent. Some of the prices are within the range of our budget so we go inside to have a chat with the owner. He said he could show us two places if we had time to accompany him.

So off we head, out through the high wall that encircles Lucca, heading to the village of Monsagrati, about 12km away, where we are shown a nice two-storey house, with a swimming pool and attractive garden.

We like it. Next stop, a little further along, is an attractive apartment, more modern, but no pool and no garden. We tell the agent we like the first one, but can't commit until we have seen the house in Greve which has virtually been reserved for us.

Off we go to Greve, about 100km further on, and book into a hotel. Next morning, as arranged, we meet our friends at the house (chateau) for rent and are taken on a tour of inspection by the owners. It really was something.

My first impression was it was a villa fit for a prince. It was an imposing three-story building with a high, wide set of steps at either end of a long patio, almost fairy-book stuff.

Then we checked out the rooms. I won't bore you with a ball-to-ball description other than to say they were a mixture of the old and the new.

The owner was a famous designer in metal, a man who could make objects of art from long tapering building nails, not just ordinary nails, but ones like those that nailed Jesus to the cross. The rooms were full of his workmanship.

The kitchen and bathroom were modern, but I felt the rest was very medieval. We moved on to the living room where another surprise awaited us. It was full of trophies, shields, pewter plates, drinking mugs, all kinds of metal… chains and wire, antique guns and pipe holders from an era long gone.

There didn't look to be much room for sitting down. The bedroom looked comfortable enough apart from the window, which really was a hole cut in the wall.

A look around outside revealed a small, neat garden that

softened the look of an establishment that, otherwise, was from a period in the past. I told my friend Bob that it certainly was an impressive place but I would have to talk it over with Lola first. I would ring him in the morning with our decision.

Bob drives to his home in Seano outside Florence, and Lola and I book in for another night in Greve. We both agreed it was an outstanding property, but there were drawbacks. Lola said she wouldn't be comfortable in such a big kitchen, and how could she keep the living room clean with so many objects to dust and polish?

But her main grievance was that there was no telephone. When this was pointed out to the owners earlier they said their daughter, who lived in an apartment on the third floor, had a telephone and would relay any messages for us. This wasn't good enough for Lola, she wanted to be on the phone to home whenever she pleased.

My view was that while it was a great place I wouldn't feel comfortable living there and, anyway, the rent was a bit too much for our budget. At 1,500,000 lire a month (less than $1,500) it was a steal for what it offered, but it wasn't the kind of home I was expecting.

Finally, it was the lack of a telephone that clinched our refusal.

I wasn't looking forward to telling Bob, because I'm sure he thought it was a done deal. How could we knock back such a mansion? I gave him the bad news over the phone but he said he understood and invited us to have lunch at his home when we were eventually on our way back to Turin.

We took him up on the offer and it turned out to be a pleasant afternoon. Bob and his wife Flo lived in quiet isolation on a hillside in Seano looking down on one of the most beautiful valleys I have seen. Eating lunch 'al fresco' in the warm autumn sunshine overlooking a little village below was one of life's little pleasures. You don't get to experience that very often.

Before we left, I thought it only proper to pay Bob a commission for all the trouble he had gone to in trying to arrange the accommodation for me. It wasn't his fault we didn't take it and after all he was in the rental business and relying on it for income. So we parted amicably with Lola inviting Flo to bring Bob for a weekend when we finally got settled.

Lola and I still had a few days to fill in before we could take delivery of the car, so we decided to see some more of the area in which we found ourselves, Chianti country.

There is a brand of Chianti wine called Ruffino, which I had tried a couple of times and found very palatable. Now I discovered myself within 50km of this historic town of Rufina, famous for its Chianti wine. Why not take a look?

It was an easy drive through the rolling hills and valleys where the grape vines stretched in endless rows, seemingly from one end of the world to the other. We passed through the outskirts of Florence to reach Rufina, about 20km further on where we booked into a delightful hotel which, unexpectedly, had undercover parking.

I mention this hotel, La Speranza da Grazzini, because it educated me to the way Italians live. They generally start their meal with antipasti, a collection of cold meats, but in this place the entrée was crostini. I had never heard of crostini, but I soon got to like it.

All it was were some rounds of toasted bread topped with mushrooms, smoked salmon, tomato, grilled cheese or fig paste. It was bit of a lottery, you never knew what you were going to get, but it was all good.

Then there was the wine. Newcomers like us bought it by the glass, but the permanent roomers had their own bottle which was kept corked in a nearby cupboard and brought out each night and placed on their table in advance.

Rufina certainly lived up to its reputation as one of the best wine growing areas in Italy, but we had to move on, so it was back to Greve for another night before heading on to Turin.

After the stop off for lunch with Bob and Flo Hope in Seano, it was on to Lucca to follow up on the rental property we had inspected, and liked, on the way to Greve. Compared to the grand villa we had inspected there this one outside Lucca was looking very attractive.

The real estate agent had invited the owner of the property to meet us in his office to discuss the terms, if we decided we wanted to rent her house. By a coincidence, we discovered the owner, a widow, Lia Cortopassi, was born in the same year as me, 1928, so we were off to a good start.

Things were looking even better when Mrs. Cortopassi agreed that we needed a telephone. She said the fittings were already in place and it only needed for the instrument to be installed. She would also provide a new washing machine for the laundry. Once these matters were settled we were well on our way to an agreement.

If we were prepared to stay for 12 months she would fix the rental at 1,000,000 lire per month, which translated to a little less than $250 a week. That sounded pretty fair to me, but to be on the safe side I suggested we fix the lease for six months, with an option to take it for a further six-month period. That proved to be satisfactory so we signed the papers and set off for Turin.

This time things went more smoothly at the Fiat factory, but there were still hassles. Before I could drive the car away I had to take out compulsory insurance. More paperwork. Then I would need petrol. The gauge was virtually on empty. 'Petrol?' the salesman queried. 'There is enough to get you outside the gates. There is a filling station just around the corner.'

I must have expressed surprise because he went on to explain. 'I'm sorry,' he said, 'but Fiat has to make money, times are hard, you can't have petrol in the tank, only enough to get you started.'

Well, what the heck. We were ready to go at last. The only concern now was how I was going to get rid of the car later after the salesman's dire predictions of all the trouble I would have. But I need not have worried.

Towards the end of our sabbatical, and when I was still wondering about how I would get rid of the car, a married couple came from Germany to rent the apartment beneath the one we occupied.

The house was divided into two—we occupied the top floor while the owner, Mrs. Cortopassie, kept the bottom one for her own use, except for the months of July and August, when holiday makers from Switzerland and Germany would pay the equivalent of $2000 per week for the three-bedroom unit.

We became very friendly with the Germans and went on day trips with them and to restaurants for dinner at night. During their stay Thomas, the husband, asked me what I was going to do with my car when we left. I said I hoped to spread the word among the locals or to advertise it if necessary.

He told me that even if I was successful it would be very difficult for me because of all the paperwork involved with transferring the registration. "In Italy they have many regulations and taxes, and unless you can speak the language very well you will need expert help.

'I can save you all that trouble,' he said. He told me he owned a Autohaus in the town of Bopfingen and his business was selling new and used cars. 'If you bring your car to me in Germany I will buy it from you,' he said. 'You won't have to do anything. Just give me the ownership papers and I will look after everything.'

This was music to my ears as I was really worried about what I was going to do. If he worst came to the worst I could always ship the car home but the cost would be prohibitive and that would negate the whole exercise of buying it in the first place.

Thomas explained it was cheaper for me to sell the car in Germany. 'In Germany you will pay 15 per cent tax compared to 19 per cent in Italy,' he said. 'In Germany a car like yours, new, would fetch around $18,000 Australian. Allowing for your mileage and depreciation and all the taxes, I could give you $10,000.'

I couldn't believe my luck. I had only paid that much for the car in the first place. So that was one big worry off my mind and I told Thomas I would bring the car to him when my time in Italy was up.

And so the holiday continued. I must say it was one of the most satisfying periods of my life, or should I say the most relaxing. I could sit all day in the sunshine or splash around in the pool. Or maybe drive to Florence for a pre-dinner drink at the Hotel Baglioni, which had a delightful rooftop restaurant overlooking the whole of the city. How could you be so lucky?

But it wasn't all play. Our apartment was part of a fairly big property with lawns to mow, the pool to keep clean, and then there was the garden. I bought tomato plants and stakes to hold them up, seedlings of geraniums and petunias to brighten up the borders. It was work, but it was also fun.

Lola and I lived as if we were part of the local community. There were two hotels nearby and we could walk to one of them any evening we felt inclined to have a taste of the local wine or a meal made from the local produce.

I practiced my basic Italian on the check-out girls at the supermarket and got onto first name terms with the chap who looked after the delicatessen. He told me his name was Caesar and pronounced it Chez-are. He called me Rinaldo.

He introduced me to the best brand of prosciutto, which was the most popular item the locals were buying. The item of choice was Prosciutto di Parma, but to get the best cut you had to add the word 'dolce' (sweet). It was so popular you could wait more than half an hour to be served.

I thought my use of the Italian language was improving until one morning at the fruit shop I was ordering various items when the proprietor said to me 'lei parla italiano molta bene.' (you speak Italian very well). I smiled back my pleasure but the grin was soon wiped off my face when a lady standing behind me said 'il parla brutto' (he speaks poorly).

37

Tasting The Local Wine

Our nearest neighbour was about 100 metres away, a nice Italian lady called Lena who lived with her partner Adriano. One morning soon after our arrival she came across and introduced herself, then invited us to dinner. They didn't speak any English so it was pretty hit and miss with a lot of sign language. Fortunately Lola and I had taken a few lessons in Italian so we got by.

It was a delicious meal of lamb and roast potatoes, and other vegetables cooked the way Italians do it with lots of rosemary and sage. But the interesting thing for me was the wine. Adriano produced a home-made bottle with a crown seal cap like you would find on a beer bottle. I was intrigued when he flicked off the cap with a bottle opener then proceeded to remove an oily substance from the neck of the bottle.

I think it had something to do with sealing the wine, a mixture of oil and vinegar, but I couldn't understand what Adriano was telling me. However it was only a few drops and once removed the wine was ready to pour. I thought it was awful. But Adriano said 'Buono, eh?' I didn't think it was good at all, but I nodded my head and said 'Si'. That was the signal for Adriano to suggest I should take a dozen.

The cost was less than $3 a bottle so I agreed, even if it was only to keep up good relations with the neighbours. When we got home Lola said it would be good for the gravy. As we got to know Lena better it turned out her brother Mario had a vineyard high up on a hillside nearby in a hamlet called Castagnori.

Then came the inevitable invitation that we all go and have lunch there and view the presents that had come in for the forthcoming marriage of Mario's daughter Giuliana. Adriano said he would drive because the road was very narrow and there were many turns. I'm glad he did because he didn't understate the situation. Each blind corner we came to Adriano slowed right down and honked the horn.

We drive right up to the cantina (wine cellar) which is like a big cave that has been hewn out of the hillside. Inside are the big stainless steel tanks holding the new wine. Sitting outside is Lena's brother Mario waiting for us. He told me the Germans took over his cellar during their occupation in the Second World War and destroyed a lot of his equipment.

Mario didn't speak English but I could understand enough to know that the cantina had been rebuilt and the wine tanks restored and refilled. To prove his point he went to a bench, found an empty tumbler and filled it from a tap at the bottom of the tank. 'Drink this,' he said in Italian, 'E buona.' I took one look at the size of the cup, filled to the top, and thought 'how will I get through this?'

I did. And it was good, as he had said. But I thought if this was going to be the tone of the afternoon I would finish up legless. Fortunately, by the time I had got the glassful down, Mario said it was time to meet the ladies and see the wedding presents.

He took Adriano and me into his house, a big rambling building with lots of marble benches and tiled flooring. The kitchen was big, but big as it was, it could hardly hold the wedding presents it contained. Italians do it big.

There was a freezer cabinet which took up almost the whole length of one wall, a vacuum cleaner, coffee machine, canteens of cutlery, elegant dinner sets, gleaming kitchen utensils, a magnificent chandelier—you name it and it would be there.

Then the big surprise. An inspection of the apartment Mario had built for the soon-to-be-married couple on the top of his own house. You walked up a winding iron staircase fixed to the outside wall of the villa onto a patio that led into the apartment. It was like walking into a 5-star hotel.

Everything was so modern and impressive. Giuliana would lack for nothing in the kitchen, bathroom, laundry, bedrooms and living rooms. And there was the magnificent view from the outside patio looking towards tiny village of Torcigliano and the mountains beyond.

Lena whispered in my ear: 'Costa 15 millione.' About $13,000 in our money. I would say Giuliana got a bargain.

Mario took me for a walk up a pine-dotted hillside behind his villa. He wanted to show me his plans for the future, how he would build holiday units for German tourists among the cypress trees on his 20-hectare property.

'Why Germans?' I queried. 'Because they like walking,' he said. 'They go hiking among the woods and the hills. More Germans come here than any other tourists. During the war these woods were full of German troops.'

He waved an arm indicating further up the mountain and took off, motioning for me to follow. It was steeper going now and the trees were thicker. Up we went, higher and higher until we must have been 2000 feet above sea level. Now the land flattened out and Mario pointed to the remains of an old stone wall, part of a former habitation. 'In the war, I was only four years old and my family came here to avoid the Germans,' he explained. 'The woods protected us because the Germans would not venture higher than our villa down below.'

It wasn't easy for me to understand Mario speaking in his own language, but I think I got the gist of what he was telling me. The Germans had raided the family villa when they occupied Italy in 1943, he told me. 'They soon discovered the wine cellar was stocked with hams and other meats hanging from the rafters, and there were sacks of flour and grain stored against the walls.

'The Germans believed these were provisions to nourish the Italian partisans who were giving them strong resistance. So they blew the place up,' he said. 'After the Americans came and liberated Italy in 1945, my father rebuilt the villa but not on such a grand sale as the previous one.'

As I write this, 26 years later, I wondered if Mario ever fulfilled his dream of building those holiday units. On the off chance, I Googled 'Castagnori' Italy. There was a site called Villa Castagnori so I hit the button and, would you believe it, up came a photo of a beautiful villa in a hillside setting—Mario's villa! At least to my eye it was Mario's villa. I recognised the villa, and, in particular, the terraced garden in front of it.

Of course I could be wrong, but I don't believe so. The setting is so distinctive there couldn't be two like it. I am convinced Mario has fulfilled his dream of developing his property and is now living in a new mansion he has brought to life from his old machinery shed. And, in the meantime, raking in the cash from the German tourists who now occupy his former home.

38

Into The Record Books

Now for a new story—the day I entered *The Guinness Book of Records*.

You won't believe this, but I am in the famous book for playing ring-a-ring-o' roses. It happened when I was living in Italy in 1994 and on a weekly shopping visit with my wife to the city of Lucca.

As we entered through the wall that encircles the city our attention was caught by a young lady sitting at a table with a large ledger in front of her. She motioned us to approach and explained she was taking entries for a 'girotondo' that would set a record for the longest human chain in the world.

She explained that Lucca was about to celebrate the 450th anniversary of the building of the stone wall that surrounds the city. The object was to gather 5,000 people to form a human circle by joining hands and walk two circuits of the wall, a distance of just on 4.2km.

If successful, this would beat the previous record for the 'girotondo piu lungo del mondo' (The longest ring-a-ring-o' roses in the world) which was set by the city of Trento in northern Italy the previous year when 3,941 people competed.

The young lady said that for a fee of 5,000 lire (less than $4) each, my wife Lola and I could join. We thought it would be a bit of fun so we signed up and were issued with yellow T-shirts and a numbered placard to hang around our neck. Because we were among the first to join I was No.40 and Lola 41.

The event took place a few days later on 7 May. By this time it had attracted 5,583 starters. At 3pm we started to walk, hand in hand. I had Lola on one side of me and an Italian girl on the other.

It was easy at first as we all settled into an even walking pace, but as we progressed the tempo quickened and your arms were stretched to their limit. Four hours and 40 minutes later it was over. A total of 5,448 participants had completed the course. It sounds easy, just walking hand in hand, but let me tell you, it was one of the most strenuous things I have done.

With so many people pulling against each other my arms felt as though they were being pulled out of their sockets. It was hot, I was sweating, thankful for a break when the chain was broken as someone pulled out to take a drink. If it was tough for me, think how hard it was on Lola. Soon after we began the second circuit she had had enough and pulled out to sit on the sidelines and watch.

So the city of Lucca had entered *The Guinness Book of Records* and as one of those who helped to create that record, I can claim to be a part of it.

39

Language Problems

For a non-Italian I think I coped pretty well with the language, but there was one occasion when I was really stumped. A few days after our arrival I was awoken by a dog barking at the front gate. When I went to investigate I found a beautiful little red cocker spaniel wanting to come in. So I opened the gate and let him in, and he dashed around making himself at home. Come around 5pm he was out the gate and off home.

This became a regular occurrence so Lola nicknamed him Ginger Mick, and the little fellow was always at our heels. Then one afternoon he took off early and I wondered what had happened to him. I wasn't left wondering too long. At nightfall there was a knock on my door and a lady is standing there asking: 'dov'e il mio cane?' (where is my dog?). This must be Ginger Mick's owner so I tell her I don't know. Then a thought strikes me.

Earlier in the afternoon I had heard a commotion at the home of my neighbour Lena who owned three dogs, one a female called Keeka. Looking across I saw Keeka was being courted by several dogs I hadn't seen before. Then the penny dropped. Mick must have been one of them. So how do I tell the lady her Mick is out chasing a bitch that is 'on heat'?

I didn't know the Italian for 'on heat', so I said words to the effect that Mick had gone to see our neighbour's dog because she 'desidera diventare sposata' (wished to get married)'. This broke the lady up and she left me still laughing to go and retrieve her pet.

Mick was missing for a few days but he came back, so I think his owner must have given up on him and let him come and go as he pleased. Mick was only a little fellow but he thought he was superman or something because he wasn't afraid of anything, well, not if it was locked up.

So he was always his cocky little self as we went on our morning walk to buy the newspaper. We had to pass the home of a big black Doberman who roamed the front garden, safely held in behind a locked gate. As we went by he would rush to the gate and bark vigorously at us. Mick would rush over and bark just as vigorously back at him, knowing full well he was protected by the gate. But one morning as the Doberman was going through his antics he struck out at the gate scratching it with his paws.

To my dismay the gate suddenly swung open and the dog rushed out, straight for Mick. Suddenly all the bluster had gone out of the little fellow and he was at my heels begging me to pick him up. Of course I did, but then I had to keep the Doberman at bay, a situation that was looking dangerous. Fortunately the commotion we created roused the Doberman's owner who rushed out and grabbed his dog by the collar and pulled him away.

We had escaped intact, but not before I received a tongue lashing from the Italian owner who was shouting words like 'stupido stranieri' (stupid foreigners). Mick and I found an alternative route to the paper shop after that, but the near brush with death didn't take the bravado out of him. Another day he took on an echidna, a little animal like a porcupine. In Australia we call it a spiney anteater. This little fellow had wandered into our garden and Mick was curious. But when the echidna rolled himself into a ball and flared his spikey quills Mick decided discretion was the better part of valour and backed off.

I was sorry to leave Mick behind when we left Tuscany but my departure was good news for his owner as she got her dog back… if only until the next group of foreigners arrived.

40

Going Racing In Italy

Lazy days under the Tuscan sun were such a luxury that I began to feel restless and look for something more exciting than idling around the pool. The journalist in me was missing the challenge of finding a story and writing about it.

So I decided to mix business with pleasure and go racing again. The nearest racecourse was Pisa, about 20km away, so that would be a good starting point.

Pisa racecourse is about the size of Werribee, near Melbourne, and it's an attractive course set in the San Rossore Parklands and is only a short drive from the Leaning Tower. I did get a story out of the meeting which I sent off to *Truth*.

The story concerned a horse called Lola Bum Bum. Imagine going all the way to Italy to find a horse with the same name as your wife—forgetting about the Bum Bum bit. Of course I had to back it, and it did run second at 20/1. The intriguing part of the race was the broadcast. I'm waiting to hear Lola Bum Bum being called, but all I hear is Lola Boom Boom, with the accent on the BOOM. Confusing, but that's the way they say it in Italian.

The most interesting thing about the Pisa racecourse is that it is adjacent to the training centre at Barbaricina. This a small village that caters for horses that come from all over Europe during the winter to take advantage of the milder climate.

The training facilities were unique to me at the time but now, nearly 30 years on, we have adopted them in Australia.

The feature of Barbaricina was four straight grass tracks, each about 1900 metres long. Horses would canter up on the soft, spongy, sandy surface until they reached the end, then turn around and do the required work on the way back.

These gallops, I was told, were used to prepare the great English champion Sir Ivor before he won the English Derby in 1968 when Lester Piggott declared him the best horse he had ridden.

More than 1000 horses were trained at Barbaricina at the time I was there. I wasn't surprised when I heard this as there were miles and miles of open spaces where horses could be exercised. In Australia now we are building up training centres, such as Ballarat, where trainers are making good use of a long, straight uphill gallop alongside the racecourse.

Trainer Darren Weir had great success using this track and he has been followed in more recent times by Matt Cumani, Henry Dwyer, Cairon Maher, Archie Alexander and Nigel Blackiston, to name just a few who have taken advantage of this new facility.

Racing (and trotting) is extremely popular in Italy and most of the big cities have a track. Rome and Milan are the biggest circuits so I took advantage of my retirement to see the Italian Derby, run at Rome's Capannelle racecourse. It's about 350km from where I was living at Monsagrati, to Rome, but at the speeds they drive at over there, the journey took only a bit over three and a half hours.

It was a pretty hairy drive on the autostrada. I was driving a little Fiat Uno while most of the others cars were either Mercedes or Audis, all flying along at 200-plus kilometres per hour. I travelled in the slow lane, doing about 100 or 120, which was fine if I didn't want to pull out to overtake.

I would look in the rear vision mirror and see that the road was clear behind me, but the moment I moved to a passing position there would be a flash of headlights behind me and a big Mercedes or Audi would appear from nowhere.

Sometimes it didn't matter, there were still two or three lanes outside me, but other times I had to duck back in as quickly as I could or else risk getting cleaned up. By the time we got to the outskirts of Rome I had had enough. My arms were aching from gripping the steering wheel so tightly.

There was no way I was going to drive through the city traffic to get to the racecourse at Capannelle. Italian drivers are bad enough on the open road, but on the city streets they are crazy.

Fortunately, I found a pleasant looking hotel in the first suburb we hit so I booked Lola and I in for the night. It proved a smart move because there was a bus right at the door to the Rome Railway Station. From there it was easy to take a train and a bus to the racecourse. I particularly wanted to see this renewal of the Italian Derby because Michael Kinane, the Irish jockey, would there.

Michael had won the Melbourne Cup on Vintage Crop the previous November and I was hoping he could give me an update on the horse so I would have an exclusive story to send to *Truth*. First thing though was to gain access to the jockeys' room to talk to him. I presented my Press credentials to the officials and was taken to a small room on the ground floor of the grandstand. I was told this was the Foreign Jockeys Room.

There were only four or five jockeys present (it wouldn't hold any more) and I recognised two of them, Michael Kinane and Lester Piggott. Michael had just finished second on the 5/4 favourite Overbury in the Italian Derby but he took time out to have a chat. He told me Vintage Crop had romped in with a race in Ireland two weeks earlier, and plans were to head back for a second crack at the Melbourne Cup.

He was quite talkative and my story made the front page of *Truth*.

Vintage Crop did come back that year for a second attempt and, according to the papers, there was quite some controversy over his run. I had returned from Italy in plenty of time to see the event, but had no involvement in reporting on it, having retired the year before.

I don't recall having any particular issue with the race, but the newspapers were critical of Kinane for racing so far out from the rail. I read later that Vintage Crop's trainer, Dermot Weld, had warned Kinane that the horse would not do its best if he let it get knocked about in the running.

According to reports, Weld was mindful that Vintage Crop was recovering from having 15 stitches inserted in a cut to his upper off foreleg, injured in a training mishap a few days before. He was concerned about the horse pulling up sound.

He need not have worried. Vintage Crop proved himself a warrior. Overcoming a slow getaway and covering extra ground in making up the leeway, he was still giving it his best to finish seventh behind the winner Jeune.

To show what a tough horse he was Vintage Crop came back for a third crack at the Cup the following year and gave a wonderful display of guts and stamina to run third behind Doriemus and Nothin' Leica Dane.

There are some horses you admire for their outstanding ability, horses that show a turn of foot that separates them from the pack. And then there are others, horses who win your admiration for their tenacity, their never-say-die spirit, and a will to win. Vintage Crop was one of those horses, and people, both in Australia and Europe, admired him for it.

Vintage Crop would not rate as one of the best horses to win a Melbourne Cup, but he is memorable for being the first northern hemisphere-trained horse to do so. And he was certainly one of the most popular. When he retired the Irish National Stud wanted him for its Living Legends paddocks and he lived out his days there as the star attraction. Such was his fame in Ireland a life-size statue was erected at the Curragh racecourse.

41

Truth Goes Into Receivership

Autumn came to Monsagrati and life there was idyllic. But the news from home was not so good. *Truth* had gone into receivership and was on the market. My son Peter, who worked there writing racing and trotting, wrote and asked if I knew anyone who might be interested in buying the paper.

I knew it would have to be someone involved in racing, and my first thought was Lloyd Williams, the el supremo at Crown Casino and a prolific owner of racehorses, as well as running the big property development company, Hudson Conway.

Lloyd, to that time, had won two Melbourne Cups, with Just A Dash and What A Nuisance, a tally he has now taken to six, second only to Bart Cummings who won twelve. I telephoned Lloyd from Monsagrati and outlined what had happened at *Truth*. Lloyd was courteous and sympathetic, but said he really wasn't interested in newspaper ownership, indicating he had enough on his plate with his existing business interests.

As we moved into the month of October Lola was expressing feelings of homesickness, and I wasn't particularly looking forward to the oncoming winter, so we decided it was time to pack up and head home. But first we had to go to Germany to offload the Fiat to our friend Thomas in the town of Bopfingen, about a two-hour drive north-east of Munich.

I really wasn't looking forward to the trip because I knew we had to go by way of the Brenner Pass, through the Alps. I imagined it would mean driving over mountains on a narrow road, something to which I have always had an aversion. But it turned out to be a piece of cake. A beautiful four-lane highway running through the mountains, not over them as I imagined.

Transferring the car to Thomas proved to be a simple matter, just signing a few papers he had pre-arranged, and collecting a pocketful of German marks equivalent to the $10,000 I had paid for the car. After an overnight in nearby Nordlingen Thomas drove us to Stuttgart where we caught a train to Amsterdam for the flight home.

Once back on home soil I looked around for something to do. It didn't take long to find it. I was approached by Mr Spiro Stamoulis, the new owner of *Truth* Sport to join his team as a consultant. He was looking for new ideas to spark up the paper and thought I could help. I went along to a few meetings with his executives, but it was plain to me nothing was going to bring the paper to life again.

There was always going to be interest in the racing guide, but with expanded coverage in *The Sun*'s daily Form Guide, and competition from *Winning Post*, it just wasn't going to be a viable proposition. The real *Truth* as I knew it died in 1995.

The urge to write however was still strong and I found outlets with several publications including *Racetrack*, *Winners*, *Winning Post*, *Harness Racer* and *Westbreed*, which kept up my interest. During this period I was going to the races regularly and meeting up with old friends. Among them was Fr. Joe Giacobbe, the founder of *Winning Post*, and an enthusiastic racegoer.

Fr. Joe knew lots of racing people and officiated at their weddings, baptisms and funerals and other special occasions.

This way he got to know the stories of their lives, and he felt they should be told as an example and incentive to others.

So he said to me one day: 'Look, I think we should write a book to tell these stories and call it *The Spirit of Racing*. I'll introduce the subjects and you'll write the copy. If we make any money it will go to the Doxa Foundation.' It sounded a good idea to me so Fr. Joe put it up to the publisher Michael Wilkinson. He liked the idea so the book got underway.

I interviewed some wonderful racing identities such as Jim Marconi, Kevin Mitchell, Mick Robins, Beverley Buckingham, John Patterson and Mel Schumacher to name a few. Their stories were sometimes funny, sometimes sad, but more often than not, they were inspirational to others.

Following the success of *The Spirit of Racing* Fr. Joe and I cooperated on a ripping book called *Fr. Joe and Pittsburg Phil's Winning Ways*. It was a story of the life of the American punter Pittsburg Phil who made a fortune backing racehorses. It also contained Fr. Joe's reflections on life and his tips on how to handle the often tricky situations that life throws up.

Once I got started on writing books I kept going, combining with champion jockey Simon Marshall to tell his life story under the title of *Hold Ya Horses* and then joining my cousin Neville Prendergast to write a book called *Tulloch v Todman*, the story of the rivalry of two great champions of the turf.

In 2009 I teamed up with photographer Colin Bull and Father Joe again to produce a book called *On Ya Bart* a tribute to Bart Cummings, who that year was aiming to win his 13th Melbourne Cup with Viewed, who had won the year before. Unfortunately Viewed failed to give Bart another victory in the race but he did finish a creditable seventh.

Bart was one of several sportsmen, including Roy Higgins,

who helped Fr. Joe when he was establishing Doxa, which he envisaged would help disadvantaged children to a better life.

With funds raised from a Sportsman's Night organised by Roy Higgins and friends, Fr. Joe established a holiday camp for the underprivileged at Malmsbury, which Bart used to refer to as 'Fr. Joe's Boys Town'.

Fr. Joe was, and still is, an entrepreneur. He is always coming up with new ideas to raise funds for Doxa, which has helped to educate many underprivileged young men and women and allow them to become outstanding contributors to our society. His most successful venture was the establishment of the form guide *Winning Post*. It became a strong competitor against *Truth* which had the best form guide in Melbourne.

Father Joe started off giving his newspaper away for free in 1987 at a time I was Racing Editor of *Truth*. *The Winning Post* gave an abbreviated coverage of the form, devoting just one line to each performance. At *Truth* we were providing ten times that much information.

I remember meeting Fr. Joe and wishing him good luck with his paper but telling him he could have 1000/1 about it succeeding. About ten years later, after *Truth* had ceased publication, and Fr. Joe had sold the *Winning Post* for $2.5 million, he reminded me of that occasion. 'I wish I had taken that bet you offered me about *Winning Post*,' he grinned. 'Don't worry Father,' I replied, 'I could never have paid anyway.'

42

Taking On A New Role

A new opportunity for me came up in 2004 when I saw an advertisement in the newspaper seeking applications to join the newly set up Racing Appeals and Disciplinary Board. Twelve people were being sought to make up the composition of the Board. I felt my involvement in the racing industry in various capacities for around 50 years qualified me for the job. So I shot in an application.

Two or three months later I received a letter from Racing Victoria to say I had been accepted. I was delighted because I wasn't too sure how a retired racing writer would stand up against people with judicial experience.

However, after being introduced to the other applicants who had been successful, I found that there was a wide variety of experience. Yes, there were legal people, barristers and solicitors, but there were also other racing people, like me, who came from various walks of life. I think everyone owned, or had owned, racehorses so there was no lack of knowledge of the sport.

I spent 10 years as a member of the RAD board hearing appeals from jockeys, trainers and other persons who had a grievance against a decision of the stewards. Not many appeals were successful, but several had their terms varied depending on the seriousness of the issue.

Generally three members heard the appeal, the Chairman, Judge Russell Lewis, and two members selected from the panel of 12. If it was a really big issue the number of members assisting the Chairman was increased to five.

Mostly the cases involved interference in races—jockeys appealing against careless riding charges, but sometimes there were issues regarding the medication of horses, the presence of prohibited substances in pre-race or post-race swabs. Once the board had heard all the evidence we would each give our opinion on what the result should be in a round table conference with Judge Lewis.

Mostly it would be a unanimous decision, nearly always in fact, but there was one occasion, I recall, when one of the panel had a contrary opinion and was not prepared to change it. Then the majority decided the issue.

I learned a lot about drugs and the way horses were medicated to get the best out them, but the most significant thing I learned was how much emphasis was put on the safety of racing. The stewards' chief object was to see that every jockey got home safely at the end of the day. Yes, they were on the lookout for horses not running on their merits also, but safety was the paramount issue.

Mostly the careless riding charges were straight-forward. The film of the race would be shown and the stewards would put their cases forward. Then the jockey, or his representative, would give evidence. It could have been the other way around but I think that's how it was. The film was shown several times and the board members would form their own view of the seriousness of the interference.

We all had the opportunity to question the stewards, and the jockey about any aspect of the race we were concerned about.

So that by the time all the evidence had been heard we were in a good position to give a considered opinion on whether the stewards had got it right.

There was rarely any doubt that interference had occurred. Blind Freddie could see a horse getting checked, or losing its position through being crossed or tightened, so the decision usually came down to the penalty.

Jockeys would argue that other factors beyond their control had contributed to the interference, such as another jockey shifting in or out, or that the opening they took was not as tight as the stewards made out. The jockeys, or their representative, would make out a case to have their suspension nullified or at least reduced.

So it would be up to the board members to make a decision. The stewards fixed the length of the suspension on whether they thought the interference was in the high-range, the mid-range, or the low-range, so, when I was there, the penalties, apart from spring carnival time, would be: high-range 18 to 30 days, mid-range 10 to 18 and low-range 10 days.

In the spring the stewards had a different formula: high-range was 14 days or more, mid-range was 7 to 14 and low-range was seven. These guidelines gave to Board members room to juggle with the penalty depending on their view of the interference. It wasn't unusual for a penalty to be shaved down by one or two or maybe three days, depending on the Board's view of the severity of the interference, or the degree of culpability of the jockey.

I think it was a very fair system well handled by the Chairman, Judge Lewis, who went to great pains to make sure everyone was given full opportunity to state their case, particularly young apprentices who might be appearing for the first time and feel overawed.

The RAD Board has since been disbanded and was replaced

in 2019 by a body called the Victorian Racing Tribunal, which is made up of members of all three codes: Racing Victoria, Harness Racing Victoria and Greyhound Racing Victoria. It is led by Judge John Bowman, a former Chairman of the RAD Board, so I know it is in good hands.

It's a funny thing but after I retired as a racing writer I became more involved with racing than ever before. First, I was asked to join the panel that selected the Scobie Breasley Medal winner for the best jockey of the season. After each of the metropolitan meeting we had to submit our vote for the best ride of the day on a 3-2-1-basis.

I enjoyed that role because it kept me on my toes watching each race with a critical eye. It didn't do my punting any harm either because I had a good grip on the form.

Not long afterwards Racing Victoria decided to recognise all the great champions of the past, horses, jockeys, trainers and others who had contributed to the history of the sport. They called it the Australian Racing Hall of Fame and empanelled a group of racing men, journalists, racecallers, and former administrators, to form a selection committee.

I received a call-up and joined people like Rodney Johnston (former VRC Secretary), Norman Carlyon (former Chairman of the Moonee Valley Racing Club), Brian Martin (racecaller), and Ray Thomas, Sydney journalist, along with racing writers from other states, so that the panel had a national outlook.

That was another interesting role because to do the job properly you had to go back in history to make sure you were familiar with all the horses and the people who had contributed so much to the sport.

Selecting the first group of horses in 2001 was a piece of cake because their records were so outstanding. The horses were (in alphabetical order) Bernborough, Carbine, Kingston Town, Phar Lap and Tulloch. If you had asked me to list them in order of merit I would have placed them a bit differently—Phar Lap, Carbine, Tulloch, Bernborough and Kingston Town.

Others will have their own opinion, and I can understand that, because I didn't see Phar Lap, Carbine or Bernborough, so how can my rankings be absolutely definitive? But you can only go on what you have read, or seen on old movie footage, and, on that basis, I think I've got it pretty right.

Another interesting part-time job that came along was an offer to be a member of a panel formed to review jumps racing. It was around the middle of 2000 or a bit before, and there were a lot of falls in the jumping races with horses having to be put down.

This created a great outcry from people associated with animal welfare, and groups of them would gather outside racecourses holding up placards demanding an end to the sport.

It got quite ugly at times, with some of the protesters hurling abuse at racegoers as they made their way into the course, but apart from that the demonstrations were peaceful enough. The racing authorities were well aware that jumps racing was on the nose with a lot of people and were determined to do something about it.

So Racing Victoria created the Jumps Racing Review Panel which was tasked with finding a way to make jumping races safer. Unless the number of falls could be reduced jumps racing was finished. I joined Pat Lalor, the former Chief Steward, David Cowlishaw, racehorse owner, and Peter Williams, Racing Victoria's Registrar, to try to find a solution.

We sourced information from all over the world, in particular looking at the design of the fences. One of the reason horses were falling in Victoria was that the jumps were made of solid brush. If a horse clipped the top of the jump it was most likely to somersault over it. This could lead to all sorts of problems, the horse itself could be badly injured, as could its jockey, and there was always the chance that other horses would be brought down.

So we recommended that a new type of jump be constructed with a soft top, something like a straw broom, which horses could brush through. It worked, but there were other factors which still had to be addressed. The number of horses falling decreased but there were still too many to satisfy the critics.

So Racing Victoria instituted a new Jumps Review Panel to approve which horses would be eligible to compete in jumping races. This meant they must have shown their trainers an ability to jump, they had to be fit and in good overall condition, and they must have performed well in trials.

As a further safety precaution riders were encouraged to ease their horse out of the race if they felt it was becoming fatigued and could not give of its best. Every jumping race is now examined by the panel and horses are either passed to race on or required to trial or undergo veterinary testing.

These measures have made a remarkable difference to the number of horses falling, and the overall safety of jumping races, for riders as well as horses. This has ensured the continuance of the sport for the present time. But the health and safety and treatment of all animals has become such a big issue in today's society that I wouldn't try to predict the future.

43

The Big Punters

I've met many big punters during my time as a reporter. Some I knew well, others only vaguely. And there were others I never met, but who had reputations as fearless bettors. I can only write with authority about those I knew personally, and the biggest punter in that category was the 'Filipino Fireball', Felipe Ysmael.

I was introduced to Ysmael not long after he came to Australia from the Philippines by his racing manager Frank Ford, a well-known bloodstock agent, who was a friend of mine. Ysmael was making a big impact on Australian racing spending lavishly on yearlings under Mr. Ford's guidance.

With a bankroll of $1 million Ysmael bought yearlings that turned out to be Always There (Victoria Derby), Divide and Rule (Stradbroke Handicap, Doomben Cup), and other good winners such as Romantic Miss, Red Diver, Silver Strike and many others.

As these horses were winning races Ysmael became hot copy for the racing writers and everyone was eager to know more about him. Ysmael, though, disliked publicity and was keeping out of the limelight. He loved a punt but didn't want to be seen in the betting ring. So he had Frank Ford and other commission agents put his bets on for him.

My best hope of getting a story out of him would be through Frank Ford so I asked him if he could arrange an interview. Ysmael was agreeable so I drove out to Dandenong where he had acquired a large property which he guarded like a fortress. There was an intercom system at the front gate at which I had to announce myself before gaining admission.

Once inside I had a pleasant lunch with Frank Ford and Ysmael, who had been nicknamed 'The Babe' by the media, and I learned something of the man himself. He had become very wealthy through his real estate and mining investments in the Philippines and had come to Australia with his wife and seven children to extend those interests. He said he loved Australia and wanted to spend as much time as he could here.

When I questioned him about his betting he said: 'Racing is only a hobby and relaxation for me. I do not want people to get the wrong impression about me. All I want from betting is a little fun.' While it may have been fun to Mr. Ysmael it was anything but 'fun' to bookmaker Bill Waterhouse who accommodated him.

On one occasion, according to what Frank Ford told me several years later, Ysmael asked him to put $500,000 on one of his horses, Silver Strike, which was due to run at Newcastle. 'I thought he must be joking,' Frank said, 'but he added that Bill Waterhouse had told him he would never refuse a big bet.'

Frank went on to say he travelled to Newcastle by train and got to the races in time to see Silver Strike open up 'in the red'. He said he approached Bill Waterhouse who said: 'What brings you to Newcastle?'

'The Babe wants to back the one you have in the red,' Frank replied.

'You can have evens,' said Waterhouse.

Frank continued: 'I couldn't say the full amount, he would have thought I was pulling his leg, so I said: "I'll have an even $100,000." When he had recorded the bet I said: "Now I'll have it again." Bill threw his hands up in the air and said, "I surrender. You go and tell The Babe that I think he is crazy".'

While all this was going on Frank had other men going around the ring getting set for whatever they could get on. 'We invested another $50,000 before the bookies refused to take any more,' he said. Silver Strike won by five lengths.

Subsequent to the Dandenong luncheon I would see Felipe at the races and we were on good terms, until I wrote an article that incensed him.

It came about when the Editor of *Truth*, Solly Chandler, became aware of how much publicity Ysmael's betting affairs were getting in the daily papers. He came to me during the 1967 spring carnival and said something like: 'Ron, give me something on this fellow Ysmael—how big he bets, the horses he backs, the sort of money he puts on them. I want a clear picture of how big he is in the racing scene. Don't hold back.'

I knew how much Ysmael hated stories about his betting. He couldn't understand what all the fuss was about because, he would say, he was just betting within his means. He could afford it, so why the big deal? But while Ysmael didn't think it a big deal, the public did. Punters would even chase him at the races just to shake his hand.

I remember him telling me he had to keep as far away from bookmakers as possible. 'If I go near them people follow me as if I am some sort of freak,' he said. That was the reason he had Frank Ford and others placing his bets for him. I knew he wouldn't be happy with a story focusing on him as a big punter, but you didn't argue with Solly Chandler, he was the boss.

So I write this story detailing some of the plunges Ysmael had executed, and of his duels with Bill Waterhouse, particularly honing in on Caulfield Guineas Day when he was having a bad run.

In those days the betting ring was a hive of activity. Bookies would call out the odds and punters would rush up calling out $5000 to $1000 or $600 to $400. Or, in Ysmael's case, his commissioner might say $30,000 to $20,000, or whatever. If you didn't hear the bet, the bookie would most likely tell you anyway.

So by the last race on Guineas Day, the Toorak Handicap, the Press Room had the mail that Ysmael was losing something to the tune of $90,000. The 'mail' was on the money because Ysmael instructed Ford to back Tobin Bronze in the Toorak to get him out. Frank told me he claimed Bill Waterhouse for a bet of $110,000 to $80,000 and it gave Ysmael a winning day when Tobin Bronze romped in by two and a half lengths.

Solly put the story on the front page and I thought no more about it until the following afternoon when the door of my office burst open and Felipe Ysmael rushes in. He is as mad as Hell. 'Ron,' he shouts as he brandishes a copy of the paper, 'what are you doing to me, I thought you were my friend?'

I think I must have looked a bit staggered because he goes on, banging his fist on my desk: 'In your country you say the pen is mightier than the sword,' he threatened, 'but in my country the sword is mightier than the pen!' I think if he had had a sword in his hand at the time he would have been tempted to use it, but fortunately for me he didn't.

Somehow I was able to calm him down, because no damage was done and he left peacefully. I don't recall having a lot to do with him after that incident but he continued racing his horses and betting on a grand scale.

At least he did until a year later, when he got into trouble with the stewards and was disqualified for two years. It happened over a race at Moonee Valley when he had two runners in the same race, Follow Me and Dalthing. Ysmael backed them both, having substantially more on Dalthing than Follow Me.

After the race, in which both horses were unplaced, Follow Me coming in eleventh, the stewards charged jockey George Hope, the rider of Follow Me, with not allowing the horse to run on its merits. Ysmael, as the owner, was also charged as being a party to the offence. Ysmael, Hope and trainer Charlie Waymouth, were all disqualified for two years.

I didn't have any close personal contact with Ysmael after this point, although I did follow his affairs actively as a reporter. He had that brand of personality that was always making news. He appealed against his disqualification to the committee of the Victoria Racing Club, which in those days heard all appeals. His appeal was dismissed.

Ysmael was hurt and disillusioned by the whole process. He put the majority of his bloodstock up for sale, although he retained some fillies and mares for breeding purposes. He returned to the Philippines but made a comeback to Australia when the period of his disqualification was up.

This time, however, he came back as an official of the Philippines Government after President Marcos had appointed him an Economic Attache. He was able to resume his racing interests and began buying yearlings again.

Two of them, Make Mine Roses and Carnation for Me, turned out very smart gallopers winning several good races between them. But the heady days of the middle '60s were over and Ysmael went quietly back to the Philippines in 1975 where he remained until he died in 1984.

44

The Great Bookie Robbery

Another big punter I knew was Michael Pitt. Michael was not so much into big numbers but into backing more than one horse in a race, sometimes two or three, if he could balance his figures to show a profit. Michael was a familiar figure in the Melbourne betting rings for upwards of 50 years. He was wasn't the biggest punter, but he lasted the longest.

Michael rarely bet in cash. All the bookmakers knew him and allowed him to bet 'on the nod'. They knew he owned a hosiery and lingerie factory in Fitzroy where he employed 300 people, so they had no worries about being paid.

Michael's method was to start at one end of the long row of bookmakers who lined the rail that divided the Members' Enclosure from the Public area and call out his bet. Then he would run along the rails calling out his bet to the other bookies before they had time to reduce the price.

It was really a sight to behold. I would be in the betting ring watching the fluctuations, when there would be this big flurry of people rushing from one end of the ring to the other. Once Michael started to bet other punters would quickly jump on his bandwagon and follow him as he made his way along the rails.

The bookies loved it because Michael was creating business for them. After Michael had placed his bet the onlookers would rush in to back the horse he had called out. The bookies would be madly writing out tickets while the punters jostled with each other to get set before the price was reduced. I can still hear the cries of the bookies calling out: 'Don't push, you'll all get on.'

In those days, mainly between the 1950s and '80s there were 1500 registered bookmakers in Victoria and there would be up to 400 of them operating on the metropolitan racecourses. Twenty or thirty of the ones who held the most money would be stationed along the rails. There were several other punters who, like Michael Pitt, had credit accounts with them so that no money changed hands on the day.

The rules were that the settling was done at the Victorian Club in Queen Street on Monday from noon. All the rails bookmakers had a table in the 'settling room' which was adjacent to the vast auditorium which also housed the bar and the billiard room. There they would meet their client and pay or receive as the occasion demanded.

Michael might not have been the biggest punter Australia has seen, but he was the most consistent. His forays with the bookies went on for 50 years, sometimes winning, sometimes losing, he just enjoyed he battle.

As an Honorary Member I was often at the Victorian Club at settling time on the lookout for a story. I would see Michael Pitt moving from table to table either collecting or paying out. Tens of thousands of dollars would change hands, probably hundreds of thousands. The perfect setting for a robbery.

How prophetic those words turned out to be! The biggest robbery in Australia's history took place there on 21 April 1976. And the bandits got away with the loot! No one has ever been convicted or jailed over the robbery, and the money, believed to be $15 million, has never been recovered.

I won't go into all the details of theft because the story has been told many times. Books have been written about it, and there has even been a television mini-series. But the robbery was of particular interest to me because it happened during 'settling', a time when I would often be visiting the Club.

Thank goodness I wasn't there that day. It must have been a harrowing experience for the forty odd bookmakers, their clerks and the punters who were forced to lie face down on the floor, while the six robbers menaced them with machine guns and automatic weapons.

I did speak to people who were there that day. One who was in the settling room at the time told me: 'We were ushered out of the room into the adjoining luncheon and billiard rooms.

'With their guns trained on us we were made to lie down between the billiard tables.

'We were told: "Don't look up, or you'll cop it." The three ladies who serve the lunches were being covered by the gunmen. One bandit said: "If anyone moves, the ladies will get it. If anyone has a gun don't think about using it."'

One bookmaker's clerk told me: 'I thought it was a joke at first, but when they started waving those guns about I knew it was fair dinkum. We were ushered into the luncheon room where Ambrose Palmer (boxing great) was sitting with a friend.

'When we were told to lie down, I heard one bloke say: "You too Am."

'They knew what they were about all right. This would be the biggest settling day of the year. Settling is on the first banking day after a public holiday. We have had three race days in the meantime, Caulfield on Saturday and Monday, and Moonee Valley on Tuesday.

'When all the bookies were removed from the settling

room, the bandits began to operate on the strong boxes carrying the bookies' money, which was to be used at the settling.

'They cut the locks with bolt cutters. Inside, all the money was arranged in canvas bags, one for each bookmaker. It would be a simple matter for the bandits to rip these bags open when they got them away. How they got them away I wouldn't know.'

The bookies had an arrangement with the security firm Mayne Nickless to pick up their cash after the races on a Saturday and deliver it back to them at the settling on the Monday.

On this occasion, because of the Easter Holiday, the cash bags would have contained money from Saturday, Monday and Tuesday. I don't know how many bags were delivered that day, but later reports put it down to 116.

No one knows how much money was really in those bags because the bookies weren't anxious to have their private business affairs exposed. The Victorian Club gave police an official figure of $1.34 million. But the talk around the racecourse was it could have been as much as $15 million.

The bandits were so well prepared that the whole operation took only 15 minutes. Yes, they got away with the loot but was it all worth it? Within ten years they were all dead. Five of them had met violent deaths, either as the hands of the police, or from fighting among themselves. The sixth member died a few years later when shot by police during a robbery.

45

The Hong Kong Tiger

The Victorian Club still functions today although not to the extent of its halcyon days at 141 Queen Street where it flourished for 60 years. About 10 years after the Great Bookie Robbery it sold its interests in the building in 1987 and moved on to new premises in the Rialto Towers in Collins Street.

Since then it has moved on to other locations, but always maintaining its two principal functions, the W.S. Cox Plate Luncheon and The Call Of The Card on Melbourne Cup eve.

I didn't visit the Club as often after it moved out of 141 Queen Street, which was only a stone's throw from the *Truth* office, but I never lost contact with it, and still have a bet with some of its members who operate at the races these days.

In 1993 The Club honoured me with its 'Services to Racing Award,' and every year since it has sent me an invitation to its W.S. Cox Plate Luncheon, where the new recipient of the Award is announced. I enjoy the conviviality of those lunches but I must admit to feeling a little overawed to see my name on the Honour Board alongside so many famous racing figures.

Now back to those big punters. The biggest of them all, before Kerry Packer came along, was Frank Duval, known as the Hong Kong Tiger. Why he got that nickname I'll never know, because his overseas business interests were confined to Japan. I didn't know him personally, but I was at Flemington in the spring of 1966 when he unleashed an avalanche of money on his filly, What Fun, to win the Oaks.

He created quite a stir in the betting ring because he would place himself in front of Bill Waterhouse's stand and call out his bet in a loud voice. First he claimed Waterhouse for $100,000 to $20,000 then, after Bill reduced the odds from 5/1 to 9/2, he came back and had $90,000 to $20,000.

But he wasn't finished. He returned a third time only to see Waterhouse had dropped the price to 4/1. It still did not deter him and he called out $100,000 to $25,000. This meant he had What Fun running for $355,000 to $65,000. There had never been betting like it seen at Flemington before. Unfortunately for 'The Tiger, What Fun was beaten into second place by Farmer's Daughter, a filly bred by my colleague on *The Sun* newspaper, Dudley Zillman.

I mentioned Kerry Packer's name in this context of professional punters, but you wouldn't class Kerry as such. He was a punter all right, but it was just a hobby with him. His biggest bets were made in the casinos where he could win, or lose, amounts up to $30 million. He was no slouch on the racecourse either. He bet in millions. On Melbourne Cup day in 1997 he invested $1 million on Might and Power averaging 5/1 for his money. Might and Power won after the bookies were forced to slash his odds to 7/2.

I used to see Kerry when I would visit Sydney for the big races, and, while he would be visible in the betting ring, I never saw him place a bet himself. He had a friend do that for him, at least he did on the days that I was there.

There were many stories coming out of Sydney detailing his wagers, so the journalists there were right onto him. They had him losing $7 million in one day at Rosehill and racking up losses of nearly $30 million with bookmaker Brue McHugh before winning it back, or some of it anyway.

Another punter I knew stood to win a fortune if Rising Fast could win the Melbourne Cup for a second time in 1955. His name was Ted Humphrey and he owned extensive grazing properties in north-east Victoria.

Ted was also well-known in tennis circles and was involved in promoting tournaments around Australia with stars like the Davis Cup players Frank Sedgman, Jack Kramer, Pancho Gonzales and others. He owned a few racehorses too, so I got to know him through doing interviews following a win at the races.

After his horse Denver Boy had won the Bagot Handicap at Flemington in 1974 beating Big Philou, he told me he had backed it from 100/1 to 40/1 and collected more than $80,000. As we were yarning he recalled that Melbourne Cup day at Flemington almost 20 years before.

It was the day Rising Fast was trying to make racing history by becoming the first horse to win the Caulfield-Melbourne Cup double two years running.

Ted had backed the double, that is, Rising Fast to win both the 1955 Caulfield and Melbourne Cups to win 250,000 pounds. He spread the bet with several bookmakers, but mainly with Sid Lyons who was one of the leaders in that field. Sid offered him 250/1 and after Ted had placed the bet Sid said to him: 'Do you want it again?' 'Yes,' replied Ted,' and double again!'

On Cup day Ted watched the race from the grandstand and had seen Rising Fast go under by three-quarters of a length to Toparoa who had bored out badly in the straight, taking Rising Fast off his course. Ted said he expected a protest, so he rushed down to the mounting yard to see what Rising Fast's trainer Fred

Hoysted, a close personal friend, had to say about it.

The excitement in the mounting yard was intense as everyone crowded around Bill Williamson to see if he would lodge an objection. But Williamson declined, telling Hoysted that it was the weight (63.5kg) that beat Rising Fast, not the interference.

When Ted heard this he said he turned to Hoysted and offered him a new car of any model of his choosing if he himself would lodge the protest. But Hoysted shook his head saying that the owner Lester Spring did not want to win the race that way.

So no protest was entered, but when Sellwood was later suspended for two months for causing interference to Rising Fast it only increased the speculation of what the result would have been had indeed a protest been lodged.

It was a very stiff penalty for that type of riding offence, but I learned later that the chief steward, Mr. Alan Bell, was incensed that his warning to jockeys before the race to keep it cleanly run had been ignored. The Melbourne Cup that year was one of the roughest on record for the amount of interference, and that was the reason Sellwood was hit with such a stiff penalty.

Sellwood did appeal the suspension, but his submissions were given short shrift by the VRC Committee and the penalty stood.

So while Ted Humphrey narrowly missed the win of a lifetime other doubles punters have been more fortunate. I mentioned Sid Lyons before as one of the bookmakers involved in this type of betting because he was a good friend of mine and we often talked about some of the big bets he had laid.

46

The 'Dream' Cups

In those days back in the 1950s and '60s, there would have been more than 100 bookmakers throughout Australia betting on the Cups double. Some of the odds they offered were astronomical getting up high as 33,000/1. The biggest bookies, like Sid Lyons, all had mailing lists and would send their betting charts all around Australia, and some, like Lyons, also distributed them in New Zealand.

Sid once he told me he bet a South Australian punter 10,000 pounds to 1 pound about Sometime and Gatum Gatum winning the Caulfield-Melbourne Cup double in 1963. 'It got up, and the punter built his dream home with his winnings,' Lyons said.

Sid also told me the story of the Queensland shearer who had a dream that Red Fury won the Caulfield Cup and that a horse called Stenelaus had won the Melbourne Cup in 1947. The shearer got hold of one of Lyons' charts and saw the odds about the double were 20,000/1, so he took a bet of 100,000 pounds to 5 pounds.

The story of the shearer's dream and his big bet soon got around to all the cattle stations and pubs up in Queensland and bets kept coming in from all over the place. Soon all the doubles bookies were hit at the long odds, and it got to the point where they began to reduce their commitments by laying off with each other.

Getting close to the Caulfield Cup the odds were still

astronomical because the bookies believed the double had no chance of success. On their early charts they had quoted Red Fury at 40/1 and Stenelaus at 500/1. But after the news of the dream got out, money kept trickling in for the double. As the races drew near the odds about the double shortened to 12,500/1. Then Red Fury surprised everybody by winning at Moonee Valley at 40/1.

The bookies began to get worried and looked to reduce their holdings even further. But they were all in the same boat, they were overcommitted. Then when Red Fury won the Coongy Handicap three days before the Cup the fat was really in the fire. The double then firmed to 'no quote' meaning the bookies wouldn't lay it at any price.

Fortunately for them however, Red Fury was scratched from the Caulfield Cup when his connections decided he would be better suited in the Melbourne Cup. They weren't far wrong, Red Fury starting at 14/1 ran third in the Cup behind Hiraji and the favourite Fresh Boy.

In the meantime Stenelaus was also showing form. He ran second to Red Fury at Moonee Valley and went on to run third in the Hotham Handicap behind Dark Marne and Hiraji. Surprisingly. Stenelaus didn't run in the Melbourne Cup as his connections believed he was better suited in an easier race on Oaks Day.

It turned out they were misguided because Stenelaus could only run third to Wandilow and the hurdler Gallant Gentleman.

Looking back in hindsight now, more than 70 years later, it does seem a strange decision because the Hotham Handicap has always been regarded as a good lead-up race to the Melbourne Cup. Several winners of the Hotham have gone on to win the Cup, and so have horses that have been placed in that race. A case in point is Hiraji, who beat Stenelaus for second place in the 1947

Hotham, went on to win the Melbourne Cup three days later.

As it transpired the bookies were off the hook, but the shearer's dream wasn't all that far out. By a strange twist of Fate Red Fury won the Caulfield Cup the following year. Stenelaus, however never competed in a Melbourne Cup.

The most famous story about a dream and the Melbourne Cup concerned the horse Nimblefoot who won the Cup in 1870. I have always been interested in the history of the Cup and that passion took me on a visit to Craig's Hotel in Ballarat in 2000 to see a painting of Nimblefoot that I was told was hanging there.

One of the hotel's part-owners at the time, Mr. Brendan Smith, told me he had been contacted by Christie's auction house in Melbourne a couple of years earlier telling him that the painting of Nimblefoot was coming up for sale and was he interested? He said he was, so he and his business partner went to Melbourne with the aim of buying the painting.

'The bidding started at $9,000 and went to $10,000. Our bid of $15,000 was accepted and we took the painting home,' he said. 'It was in its original frame and that's the way it is now. We didn't put it in glass or anything but left it the way it was. When we sold the hotel in 1999 we sold the painting with it.'

Nimblefoot has become part of racing folk-lore through his owner, Walter Craig, the original owner of Craig's Hotel, who dreamt his horse had won the Melbourne Cup, but he wouldn't be alive to see it.

Mr. Craig recounted the dream to friends the following morning, telling them he had seen Nimblefoot win the Cup, and had then walked over to his jockey to congratulate him.

According to Mr. Craig's memory of his dream he had then noticed the jockey was wearing a mourning band of black crepe on his sleeve. 'Why are you wearing that,' Craig asked. 'Oh,' replied the jockey, 'the horse belonged to Walter Craig who died three months ago.'

The next day, 17 August, Walter Craig died. The painting of Nimblefoot with the jockey wearing black mourning bands on his sleeves still hangs in Craig's Hotel.

Craig's Hotel, or to give its correct title, Craig's Royal Hotel, is also notable for its stables which occupy a section of the building. I became aware of the stables during my visit there 20 years ago and learned that they were occupied in the 1860s by Adam Lindsay Gordon, one of Australia's finest poets. He was so famous he is the only poet to have his bust placed in Westminster Abbey.

The more I learned about Gordon the more I admired him for his contribution to Australia's history. Not only was he a giant in literature circles he was also a great Australian, a policeman, a politician, and above all, in my opinion, a great steeplechase rider. At one meeting at Flemington in 1868 he rode the winners of all three steeplechase races.

I thought Gordon would be a worthy candidate for the Australian Racing Hall of Fame in the category reserved for 'Associates' and, during my time as a member of that panel, I did put his name forward.

I did get support, but not enough to have him elected. That still remains the case today. But I am pleased to say that in 2014 the Australian Jumps Racing Association admitted him to its Gallery of Champions.

47

3AW's Football Team

Aside from my job as a racing writer I also enjoyed my stints on radio and television. It was Harry Bietzel, the top football commentator, who introduced me to 3AW to give racing tips on his Saturday morning football show. Harry liked a bet and he knew that many football followers were also punters.

I liked Harry. He was jovial, enthusiastic and full of good humour. A former Reserves player with Fitzroy in the VFL, he also became Victoria's leading umpire. He had all the leading footballers on his show and it was a pleasure to mix with them.

Later on Harry got into some trouble with the Law and had to give the radio away while he spent eight months in prison.

What Harry did was wrong, but it wasn't a hanging offence in my opinion, and didn't affect my friendship with him. At the time Harry was the face of Soccer Pools in Melbourne and had the job of informing winners of their good fortune when their numbers came up. But Harry took his job a bit further by advising some of the people concerned how best they could invest their winnings and, at the same time, feathering his own nest.

Harry always maintained his intentions were honourable, but the investments didn't always work out as he intended, and some people lost money while acting on his advice. Harry came back from his time on the outer and resumed a lesser role in the media, thanks to the support of colleagues who had stuck to him despite his fall from grace. The football world also accepted him back admitting him to the Australian Football Hall of Fame.

I kept up my association with 3AW after Harry's departure and shared the microphone on Friday afternoons with Rex Hunt, who had taken over Harry's role, and Sam Newman and Bill Jacobs. It was a rollicking few minutes with Rex and Sam having a 'go' at each other and, for all appearances, acting like enemies. But it was all in good fun. Sam and Rex actually got on very well together, both having been outstanding footballers and with a great knowledge of the game.

I would give my tips for the following day's races and get involved in the football commentary when I was asked for an opinion. Even though I didn't get to see many matches through working every Saturday I did keep up with the game through television. Rex had a great following with his commentaries, which were quite outlandish from a traditionalist's point of view but were very entertaining.

Rex had nicknames for all the players and they did give his commentary a unique flavour. The one that always use to make me smile was when he would refer to Essendon's Sean Wellman as 'not a well man'. There were other quirky ones such as 'Special Fried Rice' for Carlton's Dean Rice and 'The Mediator' for North Melbourne's Troy Makepeace'. And the one that he would let roll over his tongue forever, 'Yaaaaablett' for Geelong's Gary Ablett.

Rex also had a nickname for me. He would introduce me on the program as 'Racing Ron', a nickname that has stuck with 3AW listeners. I still get it at the races today, nearly 30 years after I quit the station to take up my retirement in Italy. Someone will come up and say, 'Racing Ron, I used to listen to you on 3AW.' I spent 25 years with 3AW and loved every minute of it.

The best football commentator in my opinion was Bill Jacobs. Bill called it straight, no frills, no fuss, just an accurate description of the play. He had a clear, distinct staccato voice, that caught the excitement of the play and made for very entertaining listening. Harry and Rex were both excellent but Bill was 'old style' and that suited me best.

During this period I also had a gig with Channel 10, being part of a panel called *Racing Review*. There were six of us, Phillip Gibbs, the Sporting Director, Vivienne Smith, Clem Dimsey, Graeme Kelly, Peter Lovitt and myself. Every Sunday morning for more than 10 years we reviewed the Saturday's races and indulged in a bit of banter.

Peter Lovitt, who wrote for *The Australian*, was the most outspoken, and the most argumentative. His comments however got him into hot water one Sunday morning when he referred to champion jockey Harry White as Handbrake Harry.

This nickname was a private joke between Harry and Ron McDonell, who was foreman for Bart Cummings. Ron was a bit of a joker and at trackwork at Flemington would refer to Harry as 'Handbrake' and Roy Higgins as 'Robber Roy'. These nicknames never got beyond trackwork and were known to only a few regulars, like myself, at the early morning gallops.

But somewhere along the line Peter picked up on it and one Sunday morning dropped the 'Handbrake' line on our racing show. Harry, who was watching at home, was most upset and wanted an apology. He complained to Channel 10's boss, Sir Reginald Ansett, a keen racing man, who stepped in and suspended Peter for three months.

Unfortunately, once the nickname was out you would sometimes hear a disgruntled punter at the races call out 'Handbrake' if dissatisfied with one of Harry's rides. The nickname however, was never referred to in print as other racing writers, like me, had too much respect for Harry to mention it.

Channel 10 had the rights to broadcast the Melbourne Cup carnival for many years and, for each of the four days, Derby, Melbourne Cup, Oaks, and Final Day, the Racing Review panel would be out at Flemington giving predictions, mounting yard comments, and post-race interviews. One of my jobs was to join Bruce McAvaney in the broadcast box and give some commentary after a particular race.

I remember blotting my copybook one year when Bruce was busy calling the Hotham Handicap. I momentarily forgot where I was and called out some commentary of my own. It was 1979 and the race that year was called the Saab Quality. The VRC was forever changing the name of the Hotham depending on which company wanted to sponsor the race. It has now reverted back to being the Hotham Handicap thank goodness.

The 1979 Saab Quality was won by Karu, but my money was on a horse called Gunderman. Halfway down the straight Gunderman was throwing out a determined challenge and looked like going on to win. For some unaccountable reason I forgot where I was and called out loudly 'Come on Gunderman' just a yard or so from Bruce's microphone.

Bruce must have been startled by this rude interruption but he didn't blink an eyelid, calling the race through to its conclusion with Karu beating Cubacade and Sarfraz with Gunderman unplaced.

Of course I apologised to Bruce for my stupidity but nothing I could ever do would erase that loud shout of 'Come on Gunderman' from that tape of the Saab Quality. It became a source of embarrassment to me every time it was replayed.

48

Television Has Revolutionised Racing

The televising of races has probably been the greatest single advance for punters among all the amazing changes in technology that have taken place since I first became involved in the media in 1948.

To be able to sit at home and watch races being run live, and then see replays showing the salient points of a race like head on shots, incidents of interference, and horses being held up for a run has made a huge difference to the way we punt. Now we can even see jump-outs televised. Heaven forbid! Trainers in my early days would have nightmares if they knew such information was available to punters. Official trials were publicised, but they were rare, and you never got any information about jump-outs.

Back in the day, I would go to Flemington on a Tuesday morning to see horses gallop up the straight for four furlongs before big races like the Newmarket Handicap. But you were never given any information about who the horses were.

The only way I could find out was to ask the *Truth* trackman Des Spain if he could identity the horses. Des was a wizard. He knew all the horses trained at Flemington—well, most of them—because he would study their brands and keep a record in a notebook.

Otherwise you would see a trainer, like Bart Cummings

for instance, standing among the onlookers clocking the gallop and you could ask him. Bart would tell you, if he wanted to, but, mostly, I remember him watching the gallop and then getting away as quickly as possible to avoid being questioned.

For example, there was one day at Flemington when Bart kept the information to himself. It was the Saturday before the Melbourne Cup in 1996. Bart had received special permission to gallop Saintly on the course proper and there were quite a few onlookers including local and interstate Pressmen. I had retired but I was there as I was still doing some freelance work, including a telephone information service.

This Saturday morning was of interest to punters all around Australia because Saintly had won the W.S. Cox Plate and was one of the top fancies for the Melbourne Cup. Normally Bart would have been running Saintly in the LKS Mackinnon Stakes later that afternoon, as he had always done with his previous Melbourne Cup starters. Bart made an exception with Saintly because he didn't think he needed another run.

But the horse did need a hard hit out three days before the Cup and a gallop over 2000 metres on the beautifully manicured Flemington grass would be ideal. Bart got permission from the Track Manager to gallop on the course proper but was told to keep well away from the rails.

With his Cup jockey Darren Beadman on board Saintly took off from the 2000 metres working up speed until he really got into his work at the 1800 metres. That's when I hit the button on my stopwatch. I didn't remove my finger until he reached the winning post. Saintly had run the nine furlongs, or 1800 metres, in 1.59 seconds, a winning gallop according to my reckoning.

As was the practice at trackwork anyone who had clocked a gallop would often compare his time with someone standing close by, but Bart wasn't playing ball that morning. He was standing not far from me and I saw him being approached by the pressmen for his report and get the time for the gallop. But they didn't get a lot out of Bart. He had already put his watch back in his pocket.

I heard a lot of stories about what time Saintly was supposed to have run that morning including one report that he had run his last 1200 metres faster than the Newmarket winner that year. But I never saw any evidence of it, in fact, to this day, I have never seen any evidence of any time he ran that morning.

What I do know however, is the time I saw on my own watch. To run 1.59 for 1800 metres, wide out on the course proper, galloping alone, was remarkable. The track record for 1800 metres was 1.47.05 and the record for 2000 metres was held by Northerly in 1.59.46. On those figures what Saintly did that morning was mind boggling because he was galloping wide out on the course proper.

I went home after the gallop and made my usual 9 o'clock telephone call to the clients who were taking this service. I was able to tell them of Saintly's sensational gallop so I hope they benefitted from it.

I personally thought Saintly was a certainty. He had the form, a last-start winner of the Cox Plate, he was ideally drawn in barrier three, had a handy weight of 55.5kg, and was to be ridden by the crack jockey Darren Beadman. His gallop was the icing on the cake.

Darren gave him a super ride. He had him in on the rails just behind the leading bunch and was running fifth as they came to the home turn when Darren eased him to the outside. As they turned for home Saintly had clear running in front of him and he ran right away from the others winning by two and a quarter lengths.

Despite his good form Saintly started at 8/1, mainly because there were such big 'wraps' on the English stayer Oscar

Schindler, who had run third in the Prix de l'Arc de Triomphe. One opinion expressed in the newspapers was that Oscar Schindler had 50 lengths on the local stayers. Oscar finished fifteenth.

49

A Tale Of 6 Long Necks

There have also been some amazing changes in the way racing news is communicated since I retired. For instance, I never had the benefit of a laptop or an iPhone. I did have a portable typewriter, and it became a very important part of my equipment when I was working for *The Argus*—not just for writing stories, but also for carrying beer.

My portable typewriter was one of the largest of its kind and a bit of a handful to lug around, but it suited me because it had quite a big keyboard which made it easier to type. It also suited my colleagues at *The Argus* who soon discovered it had the capacity to carry six bottles of beer.

So on several occasions at around 10 o'clock in the evening, about an hour before we knocked off, I was designated to take my typewriter case across the road to the Duke of Kent Hotel and pick up half a dozen long necks. It was quite illegal of course, because 6 o'clock closing was in force in those days.

But, I guess, because the many employees of *The Argus* were such good customers the publican took the risk for us. It was all very surreptitious and I had to give the secret signal of three rings on the bell before the door was opened to me. Sometimes there would be only two or three of us on duty in the racing room and we would share our loot with the news room, so

I did enjoy some popularity.

Out-of-hours drinking in Melbourne was not uncommon. Pubs were not allowed to open on Sunday until around 1960, perhaps a bit before, but it was certainly out of bounds in the early 1950s. I know, because it was routine for *The Argus* racing staff to adjourn to a nearby pub in Queen Street on Sunday mornings for a pre-lunch drink.

Our leader at that time was Jack Elliott, the Racing Editor, and Jack was friends with the owner of this hotel which was popular with the racing crowd. So after giving the pre-ordained signal at the front door we were admitted to a back bar.

It was a unique little gathering, not just confined to us from the *The Argus*. Basil Conaghan, one of the leading trainers, was a regular and I remember meeting Dave Silk, a prominent racehorse owner and proprietor of Silks Night Club there. Jack Elliott always justified our visit by saying it was a great source of news, and he was right. The racing stories in Monday's Argus mostly came from there.

Some tall stories were told in that back bar on a Sunday morning and Jack Elliott was by far, the most outrageous of all the contributors. Jack had a reputation for exaggeration which earned him the nickname 'little lollies', because he only spoke in hundreds and thousands.

A typical example was the story he told of being in Sydney for the autumn carnival when he arrived at the races with no money in his pocket. At the last moment he had decided to change suits and had forgotten to transfer his wallet.

Jack couldn't spend a day at the races with no money so the first thing he did was to approach bookmaker Ken Ranger, whom he knew well, and explain the situation. 'No worries Jack,' says Ken, 'how much do you want?'

'Oh, just enough to see me through the day,' Jack replies.

Ken turns to his clerk telling him to give Jack whatever he needed out of the bag.

'And, do you know,' Jack went on with his story, 'when I walked away and counted it, there was 10,000 pounds.' *The Argus* boys in the bar, I think it would have been Tom Moon, Tom Melross, Bill Condon and myself, could hardly keep from laughing, but we let Jack get away with it, saying things like: 'Wow, how about that?'

Back at the office Tom Moon said to me 'We can't let him get away with that. We'll have to show him what 10,000 pounds looks like.'

So Tom rings one of our racing photographers, Les Gorrie, and explains the situation. He says: 'Les, do you think you could get up to The Mint (which was only a block away from *Truth*) tomorrow and see if you could get someone to stack up 10 thousand pounds in ten-pound notes for you. Then take a photograph of it and we'll show it to Jack.'

So a couple of nights later when we are all on duty, Les comes in just before knock-off time with the photograph.

'Jack,' he says, 'the boys would like you to know what 10,000 pounds looks like in 10-pound bills. Have a look at this.' So he hands Jack the photograph which shows it would have been impossible for Jack to fit the money in his pockets, no matter how many pockets he had.

We all had a good laugh, including Jack, who was a very hard man to embarrass. Later on Jack became Chief Racing Writer of the Melbourne Herald taking his tall stories with him. One of his colleagues there, Mick Davey, was a devout Catholic and went to Mass every day.

I used to chat with Mick often and one day I asked him why he went to Mass so frequently. I don't remember Mick's reply exactly, but it would have been something like this: 'It's because of the Confession, Ron. Every time Jack Elliott tells one of those tall stories of his, he turns to me and says: 'Isn't that right Mick?'

'I know he has just told a big whopper, but I have to nod my head and say, "yes Jack, that's right". I'm wearing the knees out of my pants asking the Priest for forgiveness.'

You might think that story is far-fetched but it's true. Mick was a lovely man, he was a lot older than me and lived by himself in a little cottage in North Melbourne. At the time I knew him he was Editor of Miller's Guide, a Melbourne Herald publication, and that's where he came into contact with Jack.

Mick didn't drive and Jack would often pick him up and take him to and from work. Jack had a genuine affection for Mick and they were actually very good mates.

The story of Jack Elliott and Ken Ranger reminded me of how much showmanship was associated with racing. Even if you weren't prosperous you had to *look* prosperous. If a trainer, or a bookmaker for instance, went to buy a drink, he didn't just extract a note from his wallet he pulled a roll of them from his pocket.

To me this was all part of the game—the theatre of racing. The racecourse was like a stage and we were all actors playing out our various roles.

Most bookmakers I knew, probably all of them, carried cash in their pockets. It was a sign they were successful and would always be able to pay.

To illustrate the point I will tell you a story related to me by Pearl Allen, whom you will recognise as Secretary to *Truth* Editor Solly Chandler, from our earlier story of the Voyager disaster. Pearl loved her racing and when she knew *Truth* was taking a tour to the English Derby she was desperate to come.

The trouble was she didn't have the cash for the ticket. No

problem for Pearl though. She was friendly with rails bookmaker Arch Hamilton through their common interest in music. She knew that Arch would be good for a loan.

When she approached him she said: 'Arch, I need $2000 to go on *Truth*'s racing trip to the Derby. Can you help me?'

'Sorry, Pearl,' was Arch's apologetic reply, 'I've only got $1000 on me.'

That's the way it was then. Bookmakers carried that sort of money around in their trouser pocket.

Of course Arch loaned Pearl the $2000 and she had the trip of a lifetime. She fell in love with one of her co-travellers and wedding bells were ringing. But when she learned she would have to live in Rockhampton all bets were off. Lucky for us at *Truth*, she was one of the best secretaries the paper ever had. She kept the show on the road.

50

Bust Up With Ian McEwan

Another great advance for journalists was the invention of the hand-held tape recorder. Prior to this the procedure was to use a notebook and pencil to take shorthand notes, or, if your shorthand wasn't up to speed you just did your best. I had studied shorthand and typing at night school so I used a bit of both, but the little tape recorder made things much easier.

I was fortunate enough to buy one on my assignment in Tokyo in 1969 and used it to record interviews when I came home. These little recorders weren't available in Australia until sometime later and I was the only racing writer using one for quite a while. I never had a problem with it until one day at Moonee Valley when I felt the wrath of the Valley's volatile Secretary, Ian McEwen.

McEwen had called a Press conference after the races had been called off following the running of the W.S. Cox Plate in 1975. It was a big day for the Valley as Princess Margaret was touring Australia at the time and had agreed to present the trophies for the Moonee Valley Cup and the W.S. Cox Plate. But a storm had hit the Valley quickly turning the track into a muddy mess and putting the running of the Cox Plate in doubt.

The stewards inspected the track and declared it safe. This allowed the Princess to do her duty and present the trophies. After another inspection following the Cox Plate, the stewards pulled the plug on the meeting.

Ian McEwen called the Press together to explain the situation. There must have been 20 reporters gathered around him, all the interstate boys were there as well as the locals and their notebooks were well to the fore.

After a few minutes into his story McEwen suddenly stopped and turned to me: 'What the fu*ken hell is that?' he roared.

'It's a tape recorder,' I answered.

'I don't talk to tape recorders,' he shouted, 'I only talk to pen and paper, put the fu*ken thing away.'

I remember that conversation so well because I guess it shocked me a bit at the time. But I put it down to McEwen just being McEwen. He was a pretty forceful character. And that wasn't the only time I got under his skin. After another Moonee Valley meeting had been marred by rain and the track had become a bog, I wrote a story about it in *Truth* with the banner headline MUDDY VALLEY.

Well, McEwen didn't take too kindly to that and virtually cut me off from all information about the Valley. He wouldn't talk to me for three months. Then one day at the races he was walking past, when he stopped, and came over with a bit of a grin. 'Enough of this bullshit,' he said, 'come and have a drink.' We adjourned to the committee room and after a couple of beers I found out he was human after all.

From that point on we got along very well. He had been in the job a few years and had done great things for the Valley. He had had the track reconstructed to improve the drainage and had built a new grandstand, and, in general, smartened the place right up.

He also endeared himself by putting on a three-course sit down lunch for all reporters in the Press Room. The best the other clubs could do was a pie, or a few sandwiches.

So as the years went on Ian mellowed and became quite a different fellow to the young buck who had come from New Zealand and needed anger management lessons before he could get the job done.

When he retired as Moonee Valley Secretary he took on a new role as Chairman of the Harness Racing Board. By that time I had retired and we had become good friends, even to the point where he employed me to write a series of articles for the *Harness Racing Magazine*.

51

So Much Has Changed

How much has racing changed, since I saw my first Melbourne meeting in 1948? Quite a lot actually—but the basics are still the same. Horses are still running on our major racecourses, Flemington, Moonee Valley and Caulfield and Sandown. Only the look of these places has changed.

Moonee Valley will be unrecognisable when a $2 billion redevelopment plan now underway is completed in 2026. There will be a new racetrack, new grandstand and provision is being made for the construction of 2000 apartments and townhouses. That's progress, you can't hold it back.

There are now far better facilities on all the racecourses—bars, dining rooms, comfortable seating areas. There is not a lot of difference now in the facilities for the public at Flemington compared to the Members'. Children are catered for with playgrounds and entertainment so that a day at the races can be a family affair.

When I first started going to Flemington, crowds of 30,000 were common on a Saturday afternoon. At spring carnival time this would swell to 100,000. These days, you are lucky to get 6000, or 7000 people on a normal Saturday. The spring carnival crowds are holding up but that is only four days a year.

The reason, I think, is not so much that racing has become

unpopular, just that there are so many more alternatives for people. Aussie Rules football has always been there as a competitor, but now there has been a massive growth in other sports such as soccer, basketball and rugby league.

And women's sport has taken off with girls now playing cricket and football at a high level.

I cannot believe the skills the girls have developed playing Aussie Rules. When I was kid if you threw a football to a girl she would be lucky to catch it and, if she did and tried to kick it, it went maybe a foot in the air then rolled sadly around her feet.

Now, of course, there is the live television of races, and we have legalised off-course betting through the Totalisator Agency Board. When the TAB was first introduced in 1961, there was an initial drop off in attendances, and the downward trend has continued as people have become accustomed to having a legal bet off-course.

These days you can go into a club or a pub or a TAB agency and have a bet at your ease. When I first started having a bet you had to know an SP bookmaker, and it was all rather furtive because what you were doing was against the law.

How easy is it now to have your bet and come home and see the race televised from your lounge room? You don't even have to leave home to have a bet. Just open an account with your favourite on-line bookmaker and ring the bet through on your iPhone.

It obviously suits a great many people to enjoy the races that way, you see that from the amount of money that goes through the TAB and the corporate bookmakers. Corporate bookmakers? Never heard of them until after I retired in 1993.

Remember how they started off in Darwin in the late '90s? Now they are worldwide with big operators like Ladbrokes and

Sportsbet turning over multi-millions every year.

But off-course betting will never compare with a day at the races for me. The racecourse is the whole package. You start off in the morning when you decide what to wear. Is it a day for a suit, or do you prefer something more casual, like a sports jacket and slacks? If you are going into the Public area you can wear what you like, within reason. For a Member though it is usually a suit and tie. A hat is optional.

When I was recording the prices in the betting ring for *The Argus* in the early 1950s, a hat was mandatory. I worked from the Members' side of the rails and the Secretary of Moonee Valley, Mr. W.S. Cox, insisted on hats being worn.

I had never worn a hat, so I had to take myself off to City Hatters, who had a shop under the clocks on Flinders Street Station. All *The Argus* men bought their hats there, so they pointed me in that direction.

I had never seen so many hats, so I tried a few on before selecting a narrow brim brown Trilby. I knew this was the choice of champion jockey Scobie Breasly so reckoned I would be in good company. It was a nerve-wracking job doing the betting in those days because so much depended on it.

The Argus' prices were the ones the SP bookies paid out on, so you had to get it right. *The Sun* and *The Age* had their men doing the prices also, so occasionally you would get a difference. But *The Argus* prices always held sway.

The races have always been the place to dress up for both men and women. There is an atmosphere about the races that inspires people to look their best—maybe it's a hangover from the days of Charles II of England when racing became the Sport of Kings.

Being there beats betting on your phone at home. At

the races you are meeting with people—friends, acquaintances, strangers, swapping stories, tips, gossip. You can't do that at home.

Then there are the horses, such beautiful animals. One of the reasons I like going to the races so much is that I can look at the horses before they race. It is part of the fun to try to pick the one that looks the fittest, or the fastest, or just the prettiest, whatever suits your fancy.

I like to think I can sometimes find the winner by looking at the sheen on a horse's coat, or whether it has a rib or two showing, to indicate how fit it may be. I like to watch the way a horse walks, how it carries itself, or just how it presents itself, whether it looks as though it is ready to race. Anyway, it's all in the mind of the beholder, but it's fun—and helpful.

So for me, the fundamentals of racing have never changed. The changes that have occurred have come through the evolution of time. Tracks are better prepared, some news ones have been added such as the Strath-Ayr at Moonee Valley, and the synthetic surfaces at Ballarat and Packenham and elsewhere.

There are now rules about how many times a jockey can use his whip. That's one change I cannot get my head around. How can you quantify how much faster one cut with the whip, or two, or three, will make a horse go?

Added to that, there is the distraction of a jockey having to remember how many times he has hit the horse before the last 100 metres. He should be giving his full attention to riding the horse out to the best of his ability, not doing his arithmetic.

Is the jockey who flays his whip in a close finish getting more out of his horse than the jockey riding hands and heels? Frankly, I think the day will come when whip strikes will be banned altogether, and jockeys only allowed to carry the 'persuader' for safety reasons.

Racing evolves through change. Look at the benefits that have come through progress. We now have starting stalls instead of the walk-up start; races are electronically timed instead of by a handheld watch; and we have the penetrometer and the going stick to measure the state of the track—all wonderful advancements that have enriched the sport.

But for me the greatest attraction of being there is the excitement of the race, to hear the thunder of the hooves, to experience the thrill of seeing a horse come from nowhere to get up and win. To hear the roar of the crowd when the favourite's number goes into the winner's frame; and then, the best feeling of all, presenting a winning ticket to the bookmaker.

Are horses better today? The simple answer would be to say 'yes' they are, but I really don't know. How would you measure it? By times? If you look at track records not much has changed in the past 20 years. Yes, Winx did set a new record for the W.S. Cox Plate in 2017. Yet, on the other hand, no horse in the last 30 years has been able to better Kingston Rule's record for the 1990 Melbourne Cup.

You would think times would be a good barometer to compare horses past and present. But there have been so many changes to the way tracks are prepared, it's a different ball game today. Tracks have a different profile now, a different type of grass, different surfaces. And you have to consider whether the track was rated good or heavy. And what about wind variation? I don't have a definitive answer.

For my part, I am just happy to reflect on some of the great horses of the past and wonder whether a modern-day champion like Winx could have beaten them. Horses like Kingston Town, Sunline, Dulcify, Tulloch, Tobin Bronze, Might and Power, Northerly and Makybe Diva.

All those horses won the W.S. Cox Plate, a race dubbed the weight-for-age championship of Australia, so it offers a good comparison for argument.

Winx makes an indelible impression, probably because she is the most recent. But she also had a 'wow' factor about her. She could get herself out of trouble when all looked lost, and she could come from back in the field and win when you thought she had no hope.

Tulloch will always remain my favourite horse, but what Winx did in winning 33 races in succession, including 25 Group Ones, out of a career total of 35 wins from 41 starts, is mind boggling. There is not a horse in the world, past or present, who can equal a record like that.

52

Harness Racing Was A Challenge

Now, because it is impossible to accurately compare horses of different eras, I'll get off that subject and tell you about my days as a harness racing writer. I spent upwards of ten years writing about harness racing in conjunction with my racing duties, and it was a very busy time keeping up with both sports.

They didn't spare me at *The Argus* because following an afternoon at the races I would have to butter up again and go to the Showgrounds to cover the trots. It wasn't just the work; it was the hours.

At the trots you finished late, how late depended on the stewards. After the last race, which would be around 11pm, probably a bit earlier, the stewards would compile their report. All the journalists, probably about six of us, would have to stand around cracking jokes until they were ready. Sometimes it would be well after midnight before we would be free to go home.

Yes, you could leave then, but who could refuse an invitation from the Secretary, Alan Dunn, to join him in the committee room for a few drinks? Some of the leading personalities in the industry would still be lingering there and you could often pick up some news.

Sometimes these convivial gatherings would go on past

2am and you would go home tired, but usually with a story in your pocket.

I really enjoyed the trots, perhaps because they were such a novelty to me. There were no harness races in Canberra when I was a boy, and I didn't see my first trotting race until I came to Melbourne as a 20-year-old. I was hooked straight away. The trots in those days were held at the Showgrounds, on a saucer-like track that measured only three furlongs around. That's what made it so exciting.

If you stretched your imagination a bit you could compare it with the chariot races at the Colosseum. It could really be that exciting. Because it was such a small track races got very tight on the corners, and at times and there were some bad falls.

That was the only negative but, thank goodness, it didn't happen too often. But when it did, drivers would get badly hurt and I remember one, G.D. 'Darkie' Wilson, was so badly injured I don't think he ever drove again.

The big thrill at the Showgrounds was to see horses come from way behind and get up and win. Under the handicapping system, horses were penalised 12 yards for every race they won. So the more you won the further back you went. I remember backing the mare Dainty Rose one night when she was handicapped 84 yards behind. She was so good she still won.

Dainty Rose was trained and driven by R.A. 'Bob' Parker who began his racing career as an apprentice jockey. Later on he became famous in the story of the immortal Phar Lap. It was a boyish Bob who rode the champion in his secret gallop at Geelong just before the 1930 Melbourne Cup. As I got to know more about trotting, Bob and I became good friends.

But it didn't start off that way. In fact, Parker was extremely angry with me over a story I had written in *The Argus* saying he had made excessive use of his whip in getting Dainty Rose home in a particular race. I remember the race well and can still see Parker using the whip for almost the whole last lap.

But what I couldn't see was that Parker was striking the shaft of the sulky and not hitting mare at all. He was naturally upset that I had virtually accused him of cruelty. After he had explained the situation to me I had to admit I was wrong. That incident taught me a lesson. Don't believe everything you see, or think you see.

Bob was the kindest man, and he loved his horses, particularly Dainty Rose. He demonstrated this during the Inter-Dominion Championship in Adelaide in 1954 when he was thrown from the sulky following a collision in one of the heats. Driverless, Dainty Rose bolted.

Parker lay bleeding on the track until he was picked up by attendants and rushed out of harm's way to the centre of the arena.

I saw Bob struggling with the medics who were treating him. As he was trying to break free, Dainty Rose was galloping blindly, out of control, behind the rest of the field.

After she had galloped madly for four laps of the Wayville circuit Parker was able to break free. He rushed across the arena in an effort to jump the running rail and take hold of his mare. Other attendants however headed him off and caught him a few yards from the fence.

In the meantime Dainty Rose continued galloping wildly around the track. Finally, she stopped, exhausted, after bolting seven laps and bleeding from severe cuts to her hocks. The tragedy of that situation was that no official tried to stop her and get her off the track, as would have been done in Melbourne.

At the Showgrounds there was always a 'pick-up man' employed just for the purpose of catching driverless horses and getting them out of danger.

The 'pick-up man' in Melbourne was one of the red coated Clerks of the Course, Bill Patten, who could pluck a driverless horse away from a field before you could blink. His horsemanship often drew a standing ovation from the crowd as he averted what could have been a dangerous situation.

Why they didn't have a man like Billy in Adelaide beggars belief.

Bob and Dainty Rose both recovered from their ordeal and went on to contest the Inter Dominion Championships in Sydney in 1956. Bob was a most unorthodox trainer who would ride his horses in a track gallop as a variation from the usual routine of doing circuits of the track in a sulky.

When Bob and Dainty Rose arrived in Sydney the trotting men there could not believe what they were seeing. Bob told me that after he had saddled the mare up one morning and sprinted her over a sharp four furlongs, they said he was 'mad'.

Mad or not, Bob's methods worked to such good effect that Dainty Rose was regarded as the best pacing mare in Australia at that time. She didn't earn enough points to make the final that year but another Victorian, Gentleman John, did, and he caused an upset starting at 15/1 and beating Mineral Spring, with the favourite Caduceus third.

I saw some wonderful pacers and Caduceus, who finished third in that inter-dominion of 1956, was one of my favourites. He was nicknamed the 'mighty atom' and it was appropriate because when he exploded he just blasted everything out of his way. His crowning achievement was winning the 1960 Inter Dominion Championship in Sydney before a world record crowd for harness racing of 50,346.

Harold Park had never witnessed such a night. The track

was never built to take such numbers and the crowd went wild looking for vantage points. They climbed onto every fence or railing even knocking down partitions in their desire to get a view of the race. And it was well worth it. Caduceus started off the back mark of 36 yards but he gradually rounded up the field dashing clear in the last 50 metres to defeat the Victorian Apmat.

But there was more to come. Bert Alley the driver of Apmat protested alleging interference from Caduceus. The crowd booed the announcement and the stewards gave the objection short consideration. They dismissed the protest in six minutes. The crowd would have pulled the place down if there had been any other decision so popular was Caduceus.

I mention Caduceus in particular but there were several other great pacers around in my time with that sport, and one of the best was Avian Derby. He won the inter-dominion championship in Sydney in 1952 and soon after set an Australian record when he ran a flying mile at Harold Park in two minutes.

He had a crack at another record later on when he attempted to break the record for a flying mile at the Showgrounds in Melbourne. The attempt created a lot of excitement because he was going to be paced by the well-known Melbourne thoroughbred trainer, B.W. 'Pat' Burke, a skilled horseman.

I had never seen one of these record attempts and was curious to see the conditions under which it was run. The idea was that Pat Burke, riding a racehorse, would sit alongside Avian Derby driven by Dave 'Darkie' Wilson, until they worked up top speed at a marker denoting the start of the mile to be run.

Then Burke would ease his horse half a length behind the pacer so that at no time in the attempt would he get in front. He stayed about that distance behind for the entire attempt, his close presence keeping Avian Derby up to the mark.

As the preparations for the test were being made, the Press crowded around anxious to get all the details and, according to my report in *The Argus* I saw Avian Derby's trainer, Sylvester Bray. pass a stopwatch to Dave Wilson and say: 'Keep him to 15 seconds for each furlong Darkie, he can do it.'

Fifteen seconds to the furlong! That meant a two-minute mile, considered impossible on a three furlongs track like the Showgrounds. The previous record there was 2 minutes 4 seconds set by Avian Derby's sire, Lawn Derby, at the Royal Show in 1938.

'Darkie' Wilson was one of the best reinsmen in Australia and after five furlongs Avian Derby was almost spot on to run a two-minute mile. Official timekeepers had him running the first two furlongs in 30 seconds and the next three in 44 4-5. If he had he kept that up he would have smashed the two-minute barrier.

However, he weakened slightly to come home the last three furlongs in 46 1-5 for an overall time of 2 minutes 1 second. When the time was announced the crowd of 21,000 was on its feet to give the little pacer one of the greatest ovations ever heard at the Showgrounds.

While times of around two minutes for a mile were big news back in the 1950s they wouldn't rate a paragraph in a newspaper today. The world of harness racing has moved on. The Showgrounds is gone, replaced first by Moonee Valley and now by Melton.

Harold Park was sold in 2010 for $185 million and is now a housing development. The new track is at Menangle where the Victorian, Smoken Up, ran a mile in 1.48.5. Two-minute pacers wouldn't get a look in these days.

After I left *The Argus* in late 1956 I didn't get much opportunity to write about trotting. *Truth* was noted for its Form Guide and trotting got barely a mention. So I never got to write about some of the great pacers of more recent times, like Paleface Adios, Gammalite, The Mighty Quinn, Hondo Grattan, Blacks a Fake, Popular Alm and Shakamaker to mention a few. But I have never lost my interest. Harness racing is exciting, it's spectacular, and the horses are loved and cared for by the participants as though they were family pets, as many of them are. The harness racing people, as a whole, were easier to get along with than the racing people, mainly, I guess, because the trotting industry wasn't as high-powered as racing.

Racing was, and is, big business with fortunes being spent on stallions, broodmares and yearlings to ensure that Australia remains a world leader in thoroughbred excellence. Our reputation is such that the big racing establishments all around the world, like Spendthrift and Coolmore for instance, have involvement here with studs, racing stock and personnel.

Harness racing is surviving, and it always will because the people who really run the show—the owners, the trainers and the drivers—are mostly country people, farmers and pastoralists, people who work on the land. These were the people I met while I was reporting trotting, the kind of people that form the backbone of Australia.

Epilogue

To reach this point in my story it has taken me up to September 2020 and we are in the middle of the Coronavirus pandemic. I, like others, haven't been allowed to go to the races for six months, and I wonder if I will ever go again.

But all has not been lost. Through the magnificent efforts of our medical experts, governments, racing's administrators and with the cooperation of the participants, the jockeys, the trainers, the stablehands etc, racing has continued.

Fast-forward now to 2021. The Coronavirus is on the wane in Australia, in fact it is almost non-existent, unlike in other parts of the world such as India, for instance, where more than 400,000 cases of the disease have been reported in one day.

So we are very fortunate in Australia but the future is still unclear. Will we ever get back to normal… to the pre-COVID-19 days? Only time will tell.

Crowds are being allowed back to the races as well as sporting events and entertainment venues of all descriptions. Our scientists have found vaccinations that will protect us against the-virus. All over the world people are being vaccinated so that we can look forward to the future with hope.

I will continue to enjoy my retirement and getting back to the races. The racecourse has been the hub of my life and I have missed the camaraderie I have shared there with so many like-minded people.

I've been through some historic times, the Great Depression of 1930, World War II and the Vietnam War, and have been fortunate enough to have come through unscathed, I was too young to have been affected by the Great Depression although it was very hard for my parents, especially my father.

World War II ended just before I turned 18 so I was unaffected by that conflict, other than to lose the guidance of my father for three years while he was in the Royal Australian Air Force and having to help my mother look after three young boys in scary times. By the time the Vietnam War came around in 1964 I was too old to go into the ballot for a call-up.

So I have had a fortunate life. I have lived through wars, epidemics and pandemics and survived to enjoy all the advantages this modern world has to offer. And I owe it all to racing.

Racing gave me the opportunity to meet my wife and raise a family. It has provided me with lifetime employment doing something I love. It has allowed me to do things I would never have dreamed of had I remained a Public Servant in Canberra.

Racing introduced me to the world. It has allowed me to meet, and become friends with, people of all walks of life, and, through knowing them, it has enriched my own.

Everyone makes their own choices in life and follows their own path. Taking an interest in horse racing is not the choice for everyone, but for those it is, there is a whole world of opportunity waiting. You just have to set your mind on it and make it happen.